EXPERIENCES IN TRANSLATION

TORONTO ITALIAN STUDIES

Goggio Publication Series
General Editor: Olga Zorzi Pugliese

UMBERTO ECO

Experiences in
TRANSLATION

Translated by Alastair McEwen

UNIVERSITY OF TORONTO PRESS
Toronto Buffalo London

© University of Toronto Press Incorporated 2001
Toronto Buffalo London
Printed in Canada

Reprinted 2001

ISBN 0-8020-3533-7

Printed on acid-free paper

Canadian Cataloguing in Publication Data

Eco, Umberto
    Experiences in translation

    (Toronto Italian studies)   (Goggio publication series)
    Based on lectures presented Oct. 7, 9 & 13, 1998 at the Faculty of
    Information Studies, University of Toronto.
    Includes bibliographical references.
    ISBN 0-8020-3533-7

    1. Translating and interpreting.   2. Eco, Umberto – Translations.
    I. McEwen, Alastair.   II. Title.   III. Series.   IV. Series: Goggio
    publication series.

    PN241.E26 2000   418'.02   C00-932443-7

University of Toronto Press acknowledges the financial assistance to its
publishing program of the Canada Council for the Arts and the
Ontario Arts Council.

University of Toronto Press acknowledges the financial support for its
publishing activities of the Government of Canada through the Book
Publishing Industry Development Program (BPIDP).

Contents

Preface

Under the auspices of the Emilio Goggio Chair in Italian Studies, the Department of Italian Studies of the University of Toronto hosted, as the Emilio Goggio Visiting Professor in 1998, Umberto Eco, communications expert, medievalist, semiotician, and novelist, of the University of Bologna (Italy).

During his visit to the Department of Italian Studies, Professor Eco delivered a general public lecture entitled 'Books in the Next Millennium' at Hart House Theatre on 15 October 1998. He also presented a series of three specialized lectures on the topic 'Text and Translation.' These were held on 7, 9, and 13 October 1998 in the auditorium of the Claude Bissell Building of the Faculty of Information Studies before a capacity audience. The lectures form the basis of the essays published here under the title *Experiences in Translation*. They constitute the first volume of the Goggio Publications Series.

Sincere thanks go to the members of the Goggio family who, through their generous endowment, made the visit by Professor Eco, his lectures, and the publication of this new series possible.

Olga Zorzi Pugliese
Chair, Department of Italian Studies, and
Emilio Goggio Chair in Italian Studies

Introduction

This book is based on the Goggio Public Lectures I gave at the University of Toronto in 1998. This printed version also contains many examples I was unable to give during the lectures owing to lack of time. I have also organized the material differently so that the first part deals more with personal experiences in translation while the second part is more theoretical in nature. With respect to the Goggio Lectures, this second part has been enhanced by many considerations suggested to me in the course of the Seminars on Intersemiotic Translation held at the University of Bologna over the last two years.

It may seem strange that, rather than discuss my experiences in translation from the point of view of theoretical concepts, I deal with theory only after analysing these experiences. But, on the one hand, this decision reflects the way in which I arrived at certain theoretical explanations, and, on the other, I deliberately wanted to discuss my experiences in the light of a 'naïve' concept of translation.

Every sensible and rigorous theory of language shows that a perfect translation is an impossible dream. In spite of this, people translate. It is like the paradox of Achilles and the turtle. Theoretically speaking, Achilles should never reach the turtle. But in reality, he does. No rigorous philosophical approach to that paradox can underestimate the fact that, not just Achilles, but any one of us, could beat a turtle at the Olympic Games.

People translate during business conventions and during sessions of the United Nations, and, even though many misunderstandings can arise, people of different languages agree on the fact, let us say, that the shoes of brand X are less expensive than those of brand Y, or that Russians do not approve of the decision to bomb Serbia. The majority of Christians have read the Gospels in translation (every nation in a different language), but all of them believe that Jesus was crucified and John the Baptist beheaded, and not vice-versa. Many theories of language say that no text has only one sense, but when two or more copy editors in a publishing house check the translation of a novel (or of an essay) there are cases in which all of them decide that the translator ought to be fired because his or her translation is unacceptable. Once I had to edit the Italian transla-tion of an English essay in which I read that, in the course of an experiment, 'l'ape riuscì a prendere la banana posta fuori dalla sua gabbia aiutandosi con un bastone,' that is, 'the bee used a stick to get hold of a banana put outside its cage.' Even before I checked against the original, I was sure that the translator was wrong: it was clear that the original English text spoke of an *ape* and that – since the Italian word *ape* means 'bee' – the translator thought that *ape* meant 'bee' in English too. Thus the first parameter to be applied in order to distinguish a good translation from a bad one is the one used by normal copy editors in normal publishing houses under normal circumstances – translations of poetry representing abnor-mal cases.

I apologize in advance for relying so much on common sense, but *common sense* is not necessarily a bad word. However, I also have taken into account many examples of abnormal cases.

Toronto, Milano, Bologna, 1998–2000

EXPERIENCES IN TRANSLATION

Translating and Being Translated

It seems to me that studying translation is like studying bilingualism. Any study on bilingualism is primarily performed by observing the behaviour of a child exposed to two languages, and only continuous daily observation yields sufficient data on the development of a double linguistic competence. Now, some linguists have said that such observation is possible only if (i) one is a linguist, (ii) working with bilingual children, and (iii) prepared to follow their linguistic behaviour on a day-to-day basis from the earliest stages. This means that a reliable study on bilingualism could be made only by a parent who is a linguist married to a foreigner (preferably one interested in linguistic matters).

I think that a theory of translation should meet similar requirements. If translation studies are concerned with the process of translation from a source text A in a language Alpha to a target text B in a language Beta, then translation scholars should have had, at least once in their life, both the experience of translating and that of being translated (obviously into a language they know, so they can work in close cooperation with their translator).

It may be objected that one does not have to be a poet to elaborate a good theory of poetry, that people can appreciate a text in a foreign language in which they have only a passive competence, and that in order to enjoy opera it is not indispensable to be a tenor. But, in reality, even people who have never written a poem know how difficult it is to find a rhyme or to invent a metaphor, and even people who have only a passive competence in a language have experienced how difficult it is to utter well-formed sentences in it. I suppose that an opera-goer unable to sing in tune can understand from direct experience (maybe by trying in the morning, when shaving in front of the bathroom mirror) the skills required to produce a high C from the chest.

Active or passive experience in translation is not irrelevant for the formulation of theoretical reflections on the subject. In my lectures, therefore, my primary aim is to consider certain problems that I have tried to solve, not as a translation theorist or as a semiotician interested in translation, but as a translated author and as a translator. Naturally, in reconsidering those experiences, I cannot avoid thinking like a semiotician, but this is only a secondary aspect of my lectures.

I have always avoided playing my two roles as semiotician and novelist at the same time. When I speak in public about my novels, and this is very seldom indeed, I do not talk about semiotics, and when I lecture on semiotics I never make references to my novels, for the double reason that nobody can be a good critic of himself or herself and that novelists, as well as poets, should never provide interpretations of their own work. As I have repeatedly stated (Eco 1979, 1990, 1994), a text is a machine conceived for eliciting interpretations. When one has a text to question, it is irrelevant to ask the author. But making some remarks about my experience as a translated author does not mean providing either a critical evaluation or a global interpretation of my work. I shall use myself only as a privileged witness on very marginal problems, always with regard to the choice of a word or the way to interpret a sentence.

In my novel *Foucault's Pendulum* there is, at a certain moment, the following dialogue (I have simplified matters by putting the names of the speakers at the beginning, as in a theatrical text):

Diotallevi – Dio ha creato il mondo parlando, mica ha mandato un
    telegramma.
Belbo – Fiat lux, stop. Segue lettera.
Casaubon – Ai Tessalonicesi, immagino.

This is a piece of sophomore humour, a handy way of representing the characters' mental style. The French and German translators, for instance, had no problems:

Diotallevi – Dieu a créé le monde en parlant, que l'on sache il n'a pas
envoyé un télégramme.

Belbo – Fiat Lux, stop. Lettre suit.

Casaubon – Aux Thessaloniciens, j'imagine. (*Schifano*)

Diotallevi – Gott schuft die Welt, indem er sprach. Er hat kein
Telegramm geschickt.

Belbo – Fiat lux. Stop. Brief folgt.

Casaubon – Vermutlich an die Thessalonicher. (*Kroeber*)

A literal translation in English would be:

Diotallevi – God created the world by speaking. He didn't send a
telegram.

Belbo – Fiat lux, stop. Letter follows.

Casaubon – To the Thessalonians, I guess.

William Weaver, the English translator of *Foucault's Pendulum*,
realized that this exchange hinges on the word *lettera*, which is used
in Italian both for mailed missives and the messages of Saint Paul
(the same applies in French) – while in English the former are *letters*
and the latter *epistles*. This is why, together with the translator, I
decided to alter the dialogue and to reassign the responsibility for
that witticism:

Diotallevi – God created the world by speaking. He didn't send a
telegram.

Belbo – Fiat Lux, stop.

Casaubon – Epistle follows.

Here, Casaubon takes on the double task of making the letter-
telegram pun and the reference to Saint Paul at the same time. In

Italian, the play was on two homonyms (the reference to Paul had to be inferred from the double sense of the explicit word *lettera*); in English, it is on synonyms (the reference to the current formula in telegrams had to be inferred from a quasi-explicit reference to Paul and from the weak synonymy between epistle and letter).

Can we say that this is a faithful translation of my text? Note that the English version of the exchange is snappier than the Italian, and perhaps some day, on making a revised edition of my novel, I might use the English formula for the Italian original too. Would we then say that I have changed my text? We certainly would. Thus the English version is not a translation of the Italian. In spite of this, the English text says exactly what I wanted to say, that is, that my three characters were joking on serious matters – and a literal translation would have made the joke less perspicuous.[1]   *a "sacred" term*

The above translation can be defined as ‾faithful,‾ but it is certainly not literal. One can say that, in spite of the literal meaning, it has preserved the 'sense' of the text. What is a 'sense' that does not correspond to the literal meaning? Does such a sense depend on the lexical meaning of the single words or on the meaning of a sentence? Moreover, the question does not seem to be only a grammatical one. We are dealing with a 'faithful' translation even though it also looks referentially false: the original Italian text says that Casaubon said p while the English text says that Casaubon said q. Can a translation preserve the sense of a text by changing its reference?

One could say that a good translation is not concerned with the denotation but with the connotation of words: the word *cool*, in English, denotes a physical state but in the idiom *keep cool* connotes a psychological one, so that a correct Italian translation should not be *rimani freddo* but rather *sta' calmo*. If we take 'connotation' in Barthes's sense (Barthes 1964), Weaver certainly preserved the moral or ideological connotations of the Italian original. But Weaver was also duty-bound to preserve many denotations of the original sentences: 'Dio ha creato il mondo' says that it is the case that a divine entity brought this universe into being, and no reasonable person could say that 'The Devil created the world' or 'God did not create the world' would be acceptable translations.

The word *connotation* is an umbrella term used to name many, many kinds of non-literal senses of a word, of a sentence, or of a whole text. That words, sentences, and texts usually convey more than their literal sense is a commonly accepted phenomenon, but the problems are (i) how many secondary senses can be conveyed by a linguistic expression, and (ii) which ones a translation should preserve at all costs.

Since the questions I have just listed are fundamental for every responsible reflection on translation, let me try to answer some of them from the point of view of my personal experience.

EQUIVALENCE IN MEANING

Equivalence in meaning cannot be taken as a satisfactory criterion for a correct translation, first of all because in order to define the still undefined notion of translation one would have to employ a notion as obscure as equivalence of meaning, and some people think that meaning is that which remains unchanged in the process of translation. We cannot even accept the naïve idea that equivalence in meaning is provided by synonymy, since it is commonly accepted that there are no complete synonyms in language. *Father* is not a synonym for *daddy*, *daddy* is not a synonym for *papà*, and *père* is not a synonym for *padre* (otherwise Balzac's *Le père Goriot* would be translated in Italian as *Il padre Goriot*, while it is more correct to translate it as *Papà Goriot* – but not in English as *Daddy Goriot* – and some English translations prefer to keep the French title *Père Goriot*).

Faced with all these problems, the first and easiest answer is that, in spite of much philosophical speculation, while there is not absolute synonymy for lexical items, different sentences in different languages can express the same proposition. What is the criterion for stating that two sentences in two different languages convey the same proposition? In order to realize that the sentences *Il pleut, It's raining, Piove,* and *Es regnet* express the same proposition, we ought to be able to express the constant proposition in a sort of metalanguage. Such a metalanguage would meet the requirements of that Perfect or Adamic or Universal language that so many have dreamt of over the centuries (see Eco 1993).

Such a perfect language can be thought of either in a mere mystical sense, or in a logical one. From the mystical point of view, Walter Benjamin (1923) said that translation implies a pure language, a *reine Sprache.* Since the translated text can never reproduce the meaning of the original, we have to rely on the feeling that all languages somehow converge. All languages – each taken as a whole – intend one and the same thing, which, however, is not accessible to any one of them but only to the totality of their mutually complementary intentions: 'If there is a language of truth, in which the final secrets that draw the effort of all thinking are held in silent repose, then this language of truth is true language. And it is precisely this language – to glimpse or describe it is the only perfection the philosopher can hope for – that is concealed, intensively, in translations.' But such a *reine Sprache* is not a language. Bearing in mind the cabalistic and mystical sources of Benjamin's thought (see Steiner 1975: 65), we can perceive the looming shadow of Sacred Languages, something similar to the secret Pentecostal gift. As Derrida (1985) said in his commentary on Benjamin: 'Translation, the desire for translation, is not thinkable without this correspondence with a thought of God.'

Now, it is beneficial for a translator to think that his or her desire to translate springs from this wish to grasp God's own thinking, but since this is a very private inner feeling (and there is no public way of verifying God's thoughts), can we use it as an inter-subjective criterion to assess the degree to which a translation is successful?

To pass from a private feeling to a public rule, we have to elaborate a logical model for the perfect language. This does not necessarily have to be of divine origin, but it should be rooted in the universal workings of the human mind. Moreover, its utterances should be expressible in a formalized language. This is precisely what many machine-translation scholars are postulating. There must be a *tertium comparationis* that allows the passage of an expression from language A to language B by ensuring that both are equivalent to an expression in metalanguage C. This mental language, made up of pure propositions, is currently called Mentalese.

Thus, given the three utterances *it's raining*, *piove*, and *il pleut*, they would have the same propositional content expressed in Mentalese. One may immediately object that, if such a criterion holds for simple expressions like *il pleut*, it cannot hold for poetic utterances like 'il pleure dans mon coeur comme il pleut sur la ville.' If we translate term by term in accordance with a criterion of synonymy in order to preserve the propositional content, we would probably get: 'it weeps in my heart as it rains over the town.' Under no circumstances could the two utterances be regarded as equivalent from a poetic viewpoint.

Without going that far, we might consider Jakobson's famous example (1960): the political slogan 'I like Ike' can convey a proposition *p* which also corresponds to sentences like 'J'aime bien Ike,' 'Mi piace Ike,' and even 'I appreciate Eisenhower,' but no serious person could say that these are correct translations of the original slogan. The propositional content is perhaps preserved, but the full sense of the sentence was also based on phonic suggestions as well as on the rhyme and (as Jakobson proved) on a paronomasia.

It would follow that the notion of propositional content is applicable only to very simple utterances that (unlike rhetorical figures) unambiguously represent states of the world and that are not self-reflective – that is, they do not focus our attention more on the expression than on the content level.

But, even for simple denotative senses, the postulate of a Mentalese cannot avoid the classical objection of the Third Man. If, in order to translate a text α, expressed in a language A, into a text β, expressed in a language B (and to say that β is a correct translation of α, and is similar in meaning to α), one must pass through the metalanguage X, then one is obliged first of all to decide in which way α and β are similar in meaning to a text γ in X and, to decide this, one requires a new metalanguage Y, and so on *ad infinitum*.

INCOMMENSURABILITY VERSUS COMPARABILITY

If it is impossible to speak of equivalence in meaning, one should then say that every language has its own genius (as Humboldt said) or, rather, that every language expresses a different world-view (Sapir-Whorf hypothesis).

There is no exact way to translate the French word *bois*. In English, it can be *wood, timber,* and even *woods,* as in 'a walk in the woods'; in Italian it can be both *legno* or *bosco*. In German it can be *Holz* or *Wald,* but in German *Wald* can stand for both *forest* and *bois* (see Hjelmslev 1943). Linguistic systems seem to be mutually incommensurable. Incommensurability, however, does not mean incomparability, and the proof is that we are able to compare the English, French, German, and Italian systems as far as trees and related matters are concerned (otherwise I could not have written the previous paragraph).

Suppose we are asked to translate from French to English 'la

Rifadeve

belle au bois dormant.' Certainly, mere lexical information does not say whether it would be better to translate *bois* as *wood* or as *timber* (Beauty could sleep, let us say, in a sawmill). To translate this title correctly, we cannot avoid making reference to a story (already known), to a lot of intertextual information, and to the fact that the same fairy tales can survive in two different cultures with two different titles. Only at that point can we decide not only that a correct English version should read 'Sleeping Beauty' (dropping any reference to trees) but also that Beauty sleeps in a wood, or at most in a forest, and not in a sawmill. We decide how to translate, not on the basis of the dictionary, but on the basis of the whole history of two literatures. In any case, we translate correctly and we do not mistake timber for forest.

Therefore translating is not only connected with linguistic competence, but with intertextual, psychological, and narrative competence.

Similarity in meaning can only be established by interpretation, and translation is a special case of interpretation, in Peirce's sense. To substitute a given expression with a series of interpretants means that the substituting expressions are never equivalent to the one substituted, since they can say more under a certain profile and less under another. 'Under a certain profile' means according to a given context. Is the French *maison* a good translation of the English *home*? We know that in certain contexts it is, while in others it is not. If I have to translate into French 'I feel at home,' it would be wrong to translate, 'Je me sens à la maison,' and would certainly be better to translate, 'Je me sens chez moi' – while in Italian one can say, 'Io mi sento a casa mia,' but it must be made clear that this house (if it is to be a home) must be the speaker's house.

Translations do not concern a shift from a language A to a language B (as happens with phrase books for tourists, which tell us that *home* can be translated as *maison, casa, Haus*, and so on).

Translations are not about linguistic *types* but rather about linguistic *tokens*. Translations do not concern a comparison between two languages but the interpretation of two texts in two different languages.[2]

SAMENESS IN REFERENCE

A classic example in pragmatics is the following: suppose that somebody utters the sentence 'It's very cold here'; the literal meaning of the sentence is that the temperature is low in the place where the sentence has been uttered, but in a given circumstance the sense of the utterance (which also implies the intentions of the utterer) is that the speaker wants someone to close the window. Such an interpretation presupposes cultural habits (for instance, the rules of etiquette).

Now suppose that this scene is narrated in a French novel. Marie wants to show her guests that Jean obeys her, and at the same time wants to tell Jean that it is advisable to convince their guests that it is so. Thus she says, in French, 'Il fait très froid, ici.' In a high school, the best translation would be 'It's very cold here.' But, if the translator, for some stylistic reason we are not considering now, prefers to translate, 'It's pretty windy outside,' nobody would say that such a translation has betrayed the 'deep' sense of the text (and of the situation). Thus a translation can express an evident 'deep' sense of a text even by violating both lexical and referential faithfulness.

The above example is probably rather far-fetched. But let me now consider a less improbable case. In *Foucault's Pendulum* the characters use many literary quotations – the text itself repeatedly shows them playing with cultural matters. Such an abundance of literary quotations is intended to show them as incapable of seeing the world except through their literary recollections. In chapter 57,

there is a description of a drive in the hills. The Italian original reads
as follows:

... man mano che procedevamo, l'orizzonte si faceva vasto, benché a
ogni curva aumentassero i picchi, su cui si arroccava qualche villaggio.
Ma tra picco e picco si aprivano orizzonti interminati – al di là della
siepe, come osservava Diotallevi ...

This text says that the characters go by car through the hills and
see beautiful landscapes, so that they have the impression of glimps-
ing boundless horizons 'al di là della siepe,' which should be correctly and literally translated as 'beyond the hedge.' If Weaver had
translated this way, no one would have understood what the blazes
the novel was talking about, since that hedge had not been mentioned before. It is not so for Italian readers, who know that hedge
very well, as it is a part of the intertextual milieu of Italian literature: the *siepe*, the hedge, is the one mentioned by Giacomo Leopardi
in his sonnet 'L'infinito,' perhaps the most famous poem of Italian
Romanticism. The Italian reader should understand that Diotallevi
can enjoy a landscape only through the poetical experience of
somebody else.

I told my various translators that neither the hedge nor the
allusion to Leopardi was important, but I insisted that a literary
clue be kept at all costs. I told them that the presence of a castle or a
tree instead of a hedge made no difference to me, provided that the
castle and the tree evoked a famous passage in their own national
literature, in the context of the description of a magical landscape.
This is how some translators solved the problem:

Mais entre un pic et l'autre s'ouvraient des horizons infinis au-dessus
des étangs, au-dessus des vallées, comme observait Diotallevi ...
(*Schifano*)

Doch zwischen den Gipfeln taten sich endlose Horizonte auf-ienseits des Heckenzaunes, wie Diotallevi bemerkte ... (*Kroeber*)

Pero entre pico y pico se abrían horizontes ilimitados: el sublime espacioso llano, como observaba Diotallevi ... (*Pochtar/Lozano*)

Però entre pic i pic s'obrien horizonts interminables: tot era prop i lluny, i tot tenia com un resplendor d'eternitat, com ho observava Diotallevi ... (*Vicens*)

Weaver simply translated, with an explicit reference to Keats,

... we glimpsed endless vistas. Like Darién, Diotallevi remarked ...

Thus, to preserve the psychological sense of the text (and to render it understandable within the framework of the receiving cultures), translators were entitled not only to make radical changes to the literal meaning of the original text, but also to its reference – since, in Italian, Diotallevi is said to have seen a hedge, while in other languages this is not the case. Only by this manoeuvre can the translator suggest what seems to be the 'deep' sense of the story, that is, a psychological feature of the character. But in order to make his or her decision (and I suppose that all my translators would have taken a similar decision even without my encouragement), the translator had to interpret the whole text, to decide that the characters were like this or like that.

Interpreting means making a bet on the sense of a text, among other things. This sense that a translator must find – and preserve, or recreate – is not hidden in any pure language, neither a divine *reine Sprache* nor any Mentalese. It is just the outcome of an interpretative inference that can or cannot be shared by other readers. In this sense, a translator makes a *textual abduction*, that is, the following inference: (i) the reference to a hedge looks like a curious case of possible intertextual quotation, but it may be that I am overinterpreting a mere lexical accident; (ii) if, on the contrary, I figure out a Rule according to which Diotallevi and his fellows frequently speak by literary allusions, and the reference to a hedge is a Case of such a Rule, (iii) then the reference will be no longer curious, nor accidental. The translator checks elsewhere in the novel and discovers that these three fellows really do make frequent literary allusions (the story of the Pauline epistle is another example) and decides to take the allusion to the hedge into serious consideration.

Of course, the whole history of a culture assists the translator in making relatively safe bets, in the same way as the whole theory of probability assists the gambler at the roulette table. Yet any interpretation remains a bet. One might also say that no English reader would pay due attention to that Darien, and that readers would have accepted the hedge without wondering where it came from. It is possible. Perhaps we (Weaver and I) wasted our time on an irrelevant detail. But we bet that this detail was important.[3]

TRANSLATING FROM CULTURE TO CULTURE

As has been said, translation is always a shift, not between two languages, but between two cultures – or two encyclopedias (see Nergaard 1995).

A translator must take into account rules that are not strictly linguistic but, broadly speaking, cultural. The words *coffee, café,* and *caffè* can be considered as reasonable synonyms when they refer to a certain plant. Nevertheless, the expressions 'donnez-moi un café,' 'give me a coffee,' and 'mi dia un caffè' (certainly linguistically equivalent to one another, as well as being good examples of different sentences conveying the same proposition, and satisfactory instances of literal translation) are not culturally equivalent. Uttered in different countries, they produce different effects and they are used to refer to different habits. They produce different stories. Consider these two sentences, one from an Italian novel, the other from an American one: 'Ordinai un caffé, lo buttai giù in un secondo ed uscii dal bar' (literally, 'I ordered a coffee, swilled it down in a second and went out of the bar'); and 'He spent half an hour with the cup in his hands, sipping his coffee and thinking of Mary.' The first sentence can only refer to an Italian coffee and to an Italian bar, since an American coffee cannot be swallowed in a second both because of its quantity and of its temperature. The second sentence cannot refer to an Italian subject (at least to an average one drinking an average espresso) because it presupposes a large cup containing what seems like gallons of coffee.

In any event, this is a case in which the translator can hope that even a literal translation will be enough to make a foreign reader understand what is going on. But there are trickier cases. It would seem that to translate *oui, monsieur* as *Yes, sir*, or *sì, signore* is a simple enough task. But when translating a nineteenth-century French novel, must we use *sir* (or *signore*) when *monsieur* appears in the original? Polite French people still address cab drivers as *Monsieur*, while it would seem exaggerated to use *Sir* in a similar circumstance in, say, New York. *Sir* would have to be kept if in the original text it is intended to represent a very formal relationship, between two strangers, or between a subaltern and his superior, while it seems improper (or even ironical) in more intimate circumstances. Referring to a passerby, in New York one would say *that guy*, while in Paris one would say *ce monsieur là* (*ce mec là* would already be slang). In Paris two neighbours entering the elevator together might greet each other with *bonjour, monsieur*, while in Italian *buongiorno, signore* would introduce an excessively formal note.[4]

We might say that, when translating a nineteenth-century French novel, an Italian translator ought to drop all the cases of *monsieurs* to be found in the original text. Yet if we translate, let's say, Dumas's *The Count of Montecristo*, the presence of all those *monsieurs* not only lends the story its nineteenth-century French tone, but brings into play the conventional conversational strategies that are essential if the reader is to understand the relationships between the real characters. This means that the French *monsieur* is not only a lexical item but a sort of pragmatic operator, bound up with the customs of a society. If the translation is to convey the sense of the events that took place in the days of the Count of Montecristo, it is probably necessary to translate all, or almost all, those *monsieurs*.

In the first chapters of Tolstoy's *War and Peace* (written in Russian), the characters (Russian aristocrats) speak at some length in French, as if it were their ordinary language. Since French was a foreign language for the Russian reader, it should remain so for readers of other languages too, and every translation should keep those sentences in French. Clearly the intention of the text is to show that for Russian aristocrats at that time it was fashionable to talk in French, even if it was the language of Napoleon, the enemy of their country. The rest of the text (in the original version as well as in every translation) informs the readers about the historical situation, and makes it clear that the French sentences are only snippets of polite conversation. To cite an example, at a certain point Anna Pavlovna remarks that Prince Basil does not appreciate his own sons and does not deserve them. Basil comments in French: 'Lavater aurait dit que je n'ai pas la bosse de la paternité.' Anna Pavlovna replies: 'Please don't make fun. I want to speak seriously with you.' Thus the text says clearly that what Prince Basil said in French was more or less immaterial (it was a simple *boutade*), and even a reader who does not understand a single French word can guess what is going on.

However, I think that the Model Reader of these pages (in every possible translation) should at least realize that the French sentences are in French (and not, let's say, in Swahili). If the same dialogue appeared at the beginning of the Chinese translation in an obscure Latin alphabet or, worse still, in Chinese characters, what would readers in Beijing understand? I am not wondering what they could understand lexically, but if they could realize that these characters talked in French for reasons of snobbery. I wonder if, in a Chinese translation, to render the snobbish aspect of the dialogue, one would not have had to render it in Russian, thirty years ago, or in English, today. But it would obviously betray one of the main purposes of the novel, namely, to tell a story about the French invasion of Russia.

Let me now consider a more dramatic question. How to translate the first chapters of *War and Peace* into French? There are only two possible solutions: either (i) to put the dialogue in French without any other information, or (ii) to put in a footnote saying 'en français dans le texte.' I think that – leaving aside solution (i) and considering only case (ii) – there is a difference between the experience of a reader facing a dialogue in a language that is not the same as the one in which the rest of the novel is couched, and the experience of another reader who does not sense (aurally or visually) the difference and at most receives the marginal information that there was something weird in the Russian original.

SOURCE VERSUS TARGET

The extreme case of *War and Peace* reminds us that a translation can be either target- or source-oriented. In translation, a Source text is transformed into a Target text. However, the opposition between source-oriented and target-oriented translations is frequently confused with the opposition between source-oriented or target-oriented translation theories. These are two different questions.

Target-oriented translation theories are sceptical about the possibility of ascertaining if and to what extent the target matches the source. If no word in a language is exactly the same as any other word in a different language, and languages are reciprocally incommensurable, either translating is impossible or it consists in freely interpreting the source text and recreating it. At this point what interests scholars is no longer the relationship between source and target but rather the effect of the translated text on the target culture. Such research is undoubtedly interesting for studies in comparative literature as well as for studies on the evolution of a given national culture. Humboldt was the first to speak about the way in which a translated text can change the target language, one paramount example of this being Luther's German translation of the Bible. Certain translations have obliged a given language to express thoughts and facts that it was not accustomed to express before; the translation of Heidegger into French has radically changed, over recent decades, the French philosophical style; in Italy, before the Second World War, the first translations of American writers made by Elio Vittorini (frequently very unfaithful from a grammatical point of view) contributed to the creation of a new Italian narrative style that triumphed after the war as a form of new realism. It is extremely important to study the role of translation within the context of a receiving culture, but from this point of view a translation becomes a purely internal affair of the target language, and all the linguistic and cultural problems posed by the original become irrelevant.

It is not necessary to know Hebrew to evaluate the impact of Luther's translation upon the German language, just as it is easy to see how much Vittorini's translations influenced Italian literature even without knowing English, even if by chance Vittorini invented – à la Borges – his American originals. It is not necessary to know ancient Greek to recognize the neo-classical beauty of Vincenzo Monti's Italian translation of the *Iliad* (1810). By the way, Monti knew no Greek, and translated from other translations (so that he was called 'the translator of Homer's translators').

So much for target-oriented theories of translation. But this has nothing to do with the study of the process from a source text to a target text. At this point, the source/target dialectics ought to be considered from a different point of view, already discussed by nineteenth-century authors like Humboldt and Schleiermacher: should a translation lead the reader to understand the linguistic and cultural universe of the source text, or transform the original by adapting it to the reader's cultural and linguistic universe? In other words, given a translation from Homer, should the translation transform its readers into Greek readers of Homeric times, or should it make Homer write as if he were writing today in our language? To see how this question is not nearly as preposterous as it seems, we should consider the fact that translations age. Shakespeare's text, in English, is always the same, but if modern French readers read a Shakespearean translation from the last century they feel uncomfortable and cannot take it seriously. This means that every translator, even when trying to give us the flavour of a language and of a historical period, is in fact *modernizing* the source to some extent.

FOREIGNIZING AND DOMESTICATING

The difference between *modernizing* the text and *keeping it archaic* is not the same as the one between *foreignizing* or *domesticating* it. Even if there are many translations in which both oppositions are in play, let me consider first of all the opposition foreignizing versus domesticating (see Venuti 1998).

'Jane, I find you very attractive.' Such a sentence is usually translated in cheap Italian translations as 'Jane, vi trovo molto attraente.' This solution foreignizes too much, for a double reason. First of all, the Italian word *attraente* is not a good translation of *attractive*. In any case, no Italian male would say as much to an Italian woman – he would opt for *bella*, or *carina*, or *affascinante*. Probably translators find that *attraente* sounds very English. Secondly, if in English the speaker calls Jane by her first name, this means that in Italian one should use the pronoun *tu* instead of *voi*. The *voi* can be used only if the text reads 'Miss Jane, I find you very attractive.' Thus, in an attempt to look too English, the Italian dialogue does not say exactly what the feelings of the speaker are, nor does it express the degree of familiarity between him and Jane.

Among the more ludicrous cases of exaggerated domestication, let me quote a movie that appeared in the U.S.A. in 1944, *Going My Way*, with Bing Crosby as Father O'Malley, an (obviously) Irish priest in New York. This was one of the first American movies exported to Italy immediately after the war, dubbed in the States by Italian Americans who spoke Italian with a heavy American accent. The producer thought that, in order to be understood by an Italian audience, the names of the characters should become Italian. Thus Father O'Malley became Padre Bonelli and so on. I remember that – as a naïve fourteen-year-old spectator – I wondered why in the States everybody had an Italian name. Moreover, I wondered why a secular priest (usually referred to as *don* in Italian) was called *padre*, as if he were a regular friar.[5]

An opposite case occurred with the translation of *Foucault's Pendulum*, at a point where domestication was really indispensable, while foreignization made the text incomprehensible. Jacopo Belbo, during one of his dreamlike fantasies, writes:

> Come colpire quell'ultimo nemico? Mi sovviene l'intuizione inattesa, che solo sa nutrire colui per cui l'animo umano, da secoli, non ha penetrali inviolati.
> – Guardami, dico, anch'io sono una Tigre.

The English translation reads:

> How to strike this last enemy? To my aid comes an unexpected intuition ... an intuition that can come only to one for whom the human soul, for centuries, has kept no inviolable secret place.
> 'Look at me,' I say. 'I, too, am a Tiger.'

Why a Tiger, and why with a capital letter? This passage, as well as the whole chapter, is a sort of collage of bombastic expressions from nineteenth-century popular novels. For Italian readers, 'Guardami, anch'io sono una Tigre' is a clear reference to Emilio Salgari (a popular novelist of the second half of the nineteenth century) and to a phrase pronounced by his hero, Sandokan, known as the *Tigre della Malesia*, the Tiger of Malaya, when he was faced with a real Indian tiger. I forgot to inform my translators about this intertextual joke, and they translated literally (in French, 'Moi aussi je suis un Tigre,' in German, 'Auch ich bin ein Tiger,' and so on). If they had understood the reference (but it was really a matter for sophisticated Trivia Games), they would have easily realized, without my help, that this sentence had no referential purpose (the text has no intention of saying that Belbo was a tiger or that he believed he was). This text, allegedly written by Belbo himself, shows how Belbo melancholically and sarcastically makes a Kitsch caricature of his Will to Power. Belbo could have quoted any other famous sentence from any other nineteenth-century popular novel. In

French, it could have been (much to my satisfaction): 'Regarde moi, je suis Edmond Dantès!'

ARCHAIC VERSUS MODERN

As for the opposition between modernizing the text and making it archaic, let us consider various translations of the book of the Bible called Ecclesiastes. The original Hebrew title is *Qohèlèt*, and interpreters have many problems in explaining who he (or maybe she) was. *Qohèlèt* could be a proper name, but it recalls the Hebrew etym *qahal*, which means Assembly, and thus *Qohèlèt* could be one who speaks in the Assembly of the faithful. In so far as the Greek term for Assembly is *Ekklesia*, Ecclesiastes is not a bad translation. Now let us see how different translations try either to explain the nature of this speaker in terms understandable to the target readers, or try to lead the readers to understand that he was a typical Hebrew figure:

> Verba Ecclesiastae, filii David, regis Jerusalem.
> Vanitas vanitatum, dixit Ecclesiastes. Vanitas vanitatum et omnia vanitas.
> Quid habet amplius homo de universo labore suo, quo laborat sub sole?
> Generatio praeterit, et generatio advenit; terra autem in aeternum stat.
> Oritur sol, et occidit, et ad locum suum revertitur: ibique renascens.
>   (*Vulgata*)

> The words of the Preacher, the son of David, king in Jerusalem.
> Vanity of vanities, saith the Preacher, vanity of vanities; all is vanity.
> What profit hath a man of all his labour which he taketh under the sun?
> One generation passeth away, and another generation cometh; but the earth abideth for ever.

The sun also ariseth, and the Sun goeth down, and hasteth to his place where he arose. (*King James*)

Dies sind die Reden des Predigter, des Sohnes Davids, des Königs zu Jerusalem.

Es ist ganz eitel, sprach der Predigter, es ist alles ganz eitel.

Was hat der Mensch fü Gewinn von all seiner Mühe, die er hat unter der Sonne?

Ein Geschecht vergeth, das andere kommt; die Erde bleibt aber ewiglich.

Die Sonne geth auf und geth unter und läuft an ihren Ort, dass sie wieder dasselbst aufgehe. (*Luther*)

Parole di Kohelet, figlio di David, re in Gerusalemme.

'Vanità delle vanità! – dice Kohelet –
Vanità delle vanità! Tutto è vanità!'

Quale utilità ricava da tutto il suo affaticarsi
l'uomo nella penosa esistenza sotto il sole?

Una generazione parte, una generazione arriva;
ma la terra resta sempre la stessa.

Il sole sorge e il sole tramonta;
si affretta verso il luogo
donde sorge di nuovo. (*Galbiati*).

Paroles de Qohèlèt, le fils de David, roi de Jeroushalhaîm.

Fumée de fumée, dit Qhoèlèt: fumée de fumée, tout est fumée.

Quel avantage pour l'humain, en tout son labeur,
dont il a labeur sous le soleil?

Un cycle va, un cycle vient: en perennité la terre se dresse.

Le soleil brille, le soleil décline: à son lieu il aspire et brille là.

   (*Chouraqui*)

Parole di Kohèlet, figlio di Davide, re in Gerusalemme.

Spreco di sprechi ha detto Kohèlet, spreco di sprechi il tutto è spreco.

Cos'è di avanzo per l'Adàm: in tutto il suo affanno per cui si affannerà sotto il sole?

Una generazione va e una generazione viene e la terra per sempre sta ferma.

E è spuntato il sole e se n'è venuto il sole: e al suo luogo ansima, spunta lui là. (*Erri De Luca*)

First came the Latin Vulgate, certainly influenced by the previous Greek translation of the Septuagint. At the time the translation was made, it was still evident to the reader that *Ekklesia* meant Assembly, so that the idea of a speaker in the assembly is still clear. See, on the contrary, what is done both in the Luther and the King James translations. They are clearly modernizing, and speak of a Preacher. Perhaps the one who speaks in the Assembly is not a Preacher, in the strict sense of the term. In this sense, both the German and the English translations perhaps betray the original meaning of the word, but they suggest a function recognizable to their readers.

In the fourth version, a contemporary Italian one, the translator wants his readers to understand Hebrew culture. He is, however, a Catholic scholar and is interested in orienting the interpretation of the Sacred Text. Thus he chooses the Hebrew name but is obliged to add substantial footnotes. The fifth and the sixth translations have the radical purpose of making the text as archaic as possible, in order to convey the typical flavour of the Semitic poetical style. The first four translations do their best to make clear in contemporary terms what Ecclesiastes recommended. The invective against *vanitas* is obviously against what is insubstantial and null, and the words *vanitas, vanity, vanità,* and *Eitel* suggested the right concept, at least at the time when the translations were composed. Perhaps today the original sense has been lost, and readers think of vanity as excessive care about our own physical or social appearance.

This is why, working on the original Hebrew metaphor, Chouraqui speaks of *fumée*, 'smoke,' and De Luca of *spreco*, 'waste.' They do their best to lead readers to understand the poetic atmosphere, but do not suggest the ancient sense of vanity as void and unreality – according to me – and an appreciation of their translation presupposes a knowledge of the classical ones. The last verse, both in Chouraqui and in De Luca, is syntactically tortured from the point of view of the target language (it is neither good French nor good Italian), merely in order to convey or suggest the flavour of an exotic poetical style. Both Chouraqui and De Luca are at once foreignizing the text and making it archaic.

To show how the double opposition foreignizing/domesticating and modernizing/archaizing can produce a range of possible combinations, let us see what happened with the Russian translation of my novel *The Name of the Rose*.

I did not try to make my medieval monks look modern; on the contrary, I wanted my Model Reader to become as medieval as possible. Thus, for instance, I frequently used two opposite narrative techniques: (i) either I confronted my readers with something they ought to find shocking, except that the other characters do not react in astonishment, and so readers guess that that behaviour, or thing, or event was (contrary to their beliefs) pretty normal at that time; (ii) or I mentioned something my readers should find normal, while the other characters react in surprise – so that it becomes evident that in those times that something was unusual. For instance, when Father William puts his eyeglasses on his nose, the monks look on in amazement, so that it becomes evident that at the beginning of the fourteenth century eyeglasses were not so common.

Such techniques did not create particular difficulties for my translators. But they had to tackle a harder task when dealing with the frequent quotations and book titles in Latin. It is evident that the Model Reader of my text should be eager to make an effort in order to enter a medieval abbey and to understand not only its habits and its rituals but also its language. Such a Model Reader was thought of as a Western person who, even if he or she has not studied Latin, has nonetheless heard or read Latin sentences, not necessarily in Church, but for instance in juridical expressions (after all, even a non-Catholic American hears words like *affidavit* or *subpoena* on TV).

However, Latin is more familiar to Italian, French, Spanish, Portuguese, or Rumanian readers than to Britons or Americans. For this reason, Weaver, with my approval, sometimes shortened some long quotations and nonchalantly inserted some English paraphrases. It was a process of domestication that attempted to preserve some archaic aspects of the text.

Then came my Russian translator, Helena Costiukovich. She remarked that certainly, owing to so many common etymological roots, if a Western reader, even though not a particularly cultivated one, finds a *Pentagonum Salomonis* mentioned, then he or she can at least guess that there is a pentagon having something to do with Solomon; but the same would not happen with a Russian reader, especially if the quotation is transliterated in Cyrillic characters. Moreover, Russians do not associate Latin with religion, monks, monasteries, and so on. Thus my translator suggested, and I agreed, rendering my Latin quotations in the old ecclesiastic Slavonic used by the Orthodox Church in the Middle Ages. In that way, the reader could get the same sense of distance, perceive the same aura of religiosity, as well as understand the text – albeit vaguely. Thus, in order to make the translation very archaic, it was necessary to domesticate it.

CAN A TRANSLATOR CHANGE THE STORY?

To what extent can a translation be referentially 'unfaithful'? To make this point clearer, let me rely on the classical definition of narrative texts, that is, the distinction proposed by the Russian Formalists between *fabula* (or story) and *sjužet* (or plot).

Neither story nor plot is a question of language. Both are structures that can be translated into another semiotic system, and in fact I can tell the same story of the *Odyssey*, with the same plot, by means of a linguistic paraphrase, in English instead of Greek, through a film or a comic book. In other cases, I can tell the same story of the *Odyssey* even though I partially change the plot, for instance, by starting with the events that Ulysses (in Homer's poem) tells the Pheacians about only later. However, in the original *Odyssey* there is not only story and plot but also the level of the *discourse*, that is, the so-called textual linear manifestation, or the Greek words with which Homer tells the story.

content   STORY
         ——————
          PLOT

———————————————

expression DISCOURSE

Notice that such a distinction also holds for non-narrative texts. 'I came back because it is raining' and 'It is raining, so I came back' are two discourses with the same story and two different plots, and even a poem has both a story and a plot: 'My glass shall not persuade me I am old / So long as youth and thou are of one date' tells the story of a person who will not be convinced by his or her mirror that he or she is no longer young, until certain given requirements are met. An acceptable translation in any language could even say something like 'So long as youth and thou are of one date / My glass shall not persuade me I am old' (thus changing the plot), but the translator is duty-bound to say that the unconvincing entity is a mirror and not a person or a photograph. Thus, even when translating a poem, where the discursive level plays a fundamental role (many people can say that they do not feel old when looking in a mirror, but only Shakespeare was able to put it that way), the story should be respected.

Moreover, the story should be respected at all costs in a detective novel, where the sequence of events and even the way they are organized by the plot, plays the main role. Plot and story are so important that a translation can be deemed satisfactory even though it shows scant respect for certain stylistic subtleties found in the original.

However, this principle holds true only to a certain extent. If we return to the example of Diotallevi and the hedge, we must admit that my translators did a good job even if they changed the story slightly and said in their version that Diotallevi saw something that he did not see in the Italian one.

What was the 'real' story told by that page of my novel? The fact that Diotallevi saw a hedge or the fact that he was a sort of culture snob, able to perceive nature only if filtered through poetry? In a novel, the content level is made up not only of raw physical events (the character does such and such) but also of psychological nuances, of the ideological nature of the actantial roles, and so on.

Once again the translator must decide what the fundamental content conveyed by a given text is. In order to preserve a 'deep' story, the translator is sometimes entitled to change the 'surface' one.

Let me quote an example from my third novel, *The Island of the Day Before*. This novel is essentially based on a remake of the Baroque style and includes many implicit quotations from poets and writers of the time. Naturally, I urged my translators not to translate literally but to look for equivalents in their respective literatures of the seventeenth century whenever possible.

In one chapter, the protagonist, Roberto, describes the corals in the Pacific Ocean. Since he is seeing them for the first time, he has to use metaphors and similes based on the plants, animals, and minerals he already knows, but these had to be colourful too. Roberto was perceiving a wide variety of colours and several shades of those same colours. Since verbal language does not show images or colours, the rhetorical device by which one tries to suggest visual effects through words is called *hypotyposis*: to produce a hypotyposis, I employed all the colour terms provided by the Italian lexicon, including obsolete words from seventeenth-century literature. My goal was never to use the same term twice, and thereby create, through a plurality of colour terms, the visual impression of a plurality of colours.

Consequently, my translators had to do the same in their own language. It was clear to me that different languages can have different numbers of terms for the same colour: for instance, a given language X may have ten terms for red and only five for yellow, while – let us say – in my novel I named six varieties of yellow and only nine varieties of red. Thus I encouraged my translators to change colours freely when they ran out of synonyms. That a given coral or fish was red or yellow was not important (in those seas, corals and fish come in all colours); what counted was that the same term would not be repeated in the same context and that the reader, like the character, experienced extraordinary chromatic variety through lexical variety.

Here is my original text and the solutions of four translators:

Forse, a furia di trattenere il fiato, si era obnubilato, l'acqua che gli stava invadendo la maschera gli confondeva le forme e le sfumature. Aveva messo fuori la testa per dare aria ai polmoni, e aveva ripreso a galleggiare ai bordi dell'argine, seguendone anfratti e spezzature, là dove si aprivano corridoi di cretone in cui si infilavano arlecchini avvinati, mentre su di un balzo vedeva riposare, mosso da lento respiro e agitare di chele, un gambero crestato di fior di latte, sopra una rete di coralli (questi simili a quelli che conosceva, ma disposti come il cacio di fra' Stefano, che non finisce mai).

Quello che vedeva ora non era un pesce, ma neppure una foglia, certo era cosa vivente, come due larghe fette di materia albicante, bordate di chermisi, e un ventaglio di piume; e là dove ci si sarebbero attesi degli occhi, due corna di ceralacca agitata.

Polipi soriani, che nel loro vermicolare lubrico rivelavano l'incarnatino di un grande labbro centrale, sfioravano piantagioni di mentule albine con il glande d'amaranto; pesciolini rosati e picchiettati di ulivigno sfioravano cavolfiori cenerognoli spruzzolati di scarlattino, tuberi tigrati di ramature negricanti ... E poi si vedeva il fegato poroso colour colchico di un grande animale, oppure un fuoco artificiale di rabeschi argento vivo, ispidumi di spine gocciolate di sanguigno e infine una sorta di calice di flaccida madreperla ...

Perhaps, holding his breath so long, he had grown befuddled, and the water entering his mask blurred shapes and hues. He thrust his head up to let air into his lungs, and resumed floating along the edge of the barrier, following its rifts and anfracts, past corridors of chalk in which vinous harlequins were stuck, while on a promontory he saw reposing, stirred by slow respiration and a waving of claws, a lobster crested with whey over a coral net (this coral looked like the coral he knew, but was spread out like the legendary cheese of Fra Stefano, which never ends).

What he saw now was not a fish, nor was it a leaf; certainly it was a living thing, like two broad slices of whitish matter edged in crimson and with a feather fan; and where you would have expected eyes there were two horns of whipped sealing-wax.

Cypress-polyps, which in their vermicular writhing revealed the rosy colour of a great central lip, stroked plantations of albino phalli with amaranth glandes; pink minnows dotted with olive grazed ashen cauliflowers sprayed with scarlet striped tubers of blackening copper ... And, then he could see the porous, saffron liver of a great animal, or else an artificial fire of mercury arabesques, wisps of thorns dripping sanguine and finally a kind of chalice of flaccid mother-of-pearl ... (*Weaver*)

Peut-être, à force de retenir son souffle, s'était-il obnubilé, l'eau qui envahissait son masque lui brouillait-elle les formes et les nuances. Il avait mis sa tête à l'air pour emplir ses poumons, et avait recommencé de flotter sur les bords de la barrière, à suivre les anfractuosités et les trouées où s'ouvraient des couloirs de cretonne dans lesquels se faufilaient des arlequins ivres, tandis qu'au-dessus d'un escarpement il voyait se reposer, animé de lente respiration et remuement de pinces, un homard crêté de mozzarella, surplombant un lacis de coraux (ceux-ci semblables à ceux-là qu'il connaissait, mais disposés comme le fromage de Frère Etienne, qui ne finit jamais).

Ce qu'il voyait maintenant n'était pas un poisson, mais pas non plus une feuille, à coup sûr une chose vive, telles deux larges tranches de matière blanchâtre, bordées de rouge de kermès, et un éventail de plumes; et là où l'on aurait attendu des yeux, s'agitaient deux cornes de cire à cacheter.

Des polypes ocellés, qui dans leur grouillement vermiculaire et lubrifié révélaient l'incarnadin d'une grande lèvre centrale, effleuraient des plantations d'olothuries albuginées au gland de passe-velours; de petits poissons rosés et piquetés d'olivette effleuraient des choux-fleurs cendreux éclaboussés d'écarlate, des tubercules tigrés de ramures fuligineuses ... Et puis on voyait le foie poreux couleur colchique d'un grand animal, ou encore un feu d'artifice d'arabesques vif-argent, des hispidités d'épines dégouttantes de rouge sang et enfin une sorte de calice de nacre flasque ... (*Schifano*)

Vielleicht hatte sich infolge des langen Atemanhaltens sein Blick getrübt, oder das in die Maske eindringende Wasser ließ die Formen und Farbtöne vor seinen Augen verschwimmen. Er hob den Kopf und reckte ihn hoch, um sich die Lunge mit frischer Luft zu füllen, und schwamm dann weiter am Rand des unterseelschen Abgrunds entlang, vorbei an Schluchten und Schründen und Spalten, in denen sich weinselige Harlekine tummelten, während reglos auf einem Felsvorsprung, bewegt nur durch langsames Atmen und Scherenschwenken, ein Hummer hockte mit einem Kamm wie aus Sahne, lauernd über einem Netzgeflecht von Korallen (diese gleich denen, die Roberto schon kannte, aber angeordnet wie Bruder Stephans Hefepilz, der nie endet).

Was er jetzt sah, war kein Fisch, aber auch kein Blatt, es war gewiß etwas Lebendiges: zwei große Scheiben weißlicher Materie, karmesinrot gerändert, mit einem fächerförmigen Federbusch; und wo man Augen erwartet hätte, zwei umhertastende Hörner aus Siegellack.

Getigerte Polypen, die im glitschigen Wurmgeschlinge ihrer Tentakel das Fleischrot einer großen zentralen Lippe enthüllten, streiften Plantagen albinoweißer Phalli mit amarantroter Eichel; rosarot und olivbraun gefleckte Fischchen streiften aschgraue Blumenkohlköpfe mit scharlachroten Pünktchen und gelblich geflammte Knollen schwärzlichen Astwerks ... Und welter sah man die lilarote poröse Leber eines großen Tiers oder auch ein Feuerwerk von quecksilbrigen Arabesken, Nadelkissen voll bluttriefender Dornen und schließlich eine Art Kelch aus mattem Perlmutt ... (*Kroeber*)

Quizà, a fuer de contener la respiración, habíase obnubilado, el agua le estaba invadiendo la máscara, confundíale formas y matices. Había sacado la cabeza para dar aire a los pulmones, y había vuelto a sobrenadar al borde del dique, siguiendo anfractos y quebradas, allá donde se abrían pasillos de greda en los que introducíanse arlequines envinados, mientras sobre un peñasco veía descavsar, movido por una lenta repíración y agitar de pinzas, un cangrejo con cresta nacarada, encima

de una red de corales (éstos similares a los que conocía, pero dispuestos
como panes y peces, que no se acaban nunca).

Lo que veía ahora no era un pez, mas ni siquiera una hoja, sin duda
era algo vivo, corno dos anchas rebanadas de materia albicante, bor-
dadas de carmesí, y un abanico de plumas; y allá donde nos habríamos
esperado los ojos, dos cuernos de lacre agitado.

Pólipos sirios, que en su vermicular lúbrico manifestaban el
encarnadino de un gran labio central, acariciaban planteles de méntulas
albinas con el glande de amaranto; pececillos rosados y jaspeados de
aceituní acariciaban coliflores cenicientas sembradas de escarlata,
raigones listados de cobre negreante ... Y luego veíse el hígado poroso
color cólquico de un gran aminal, o un fuego artificial de arabescos de
plata viva, hispidumbres de espinas salpicadas de sangriento y, for fin,
una suerte de cáliz de fláccida madreperla ... (*Lozano*)

Even though one can say that all the translators did their best to
respect my chromatic suggestions, one can see that when I said that
there was a sort of porous liver *color colchico* (the colour of an
autumn crocus), I left the colour undetermined, since crocus leaves
can be yellow, lilac, or whatever. Weaver chose *saffron*, Kroeber
lilarote. Weaver speaks of cypress-polyps, Lozano of *pólipos sirios*,
and Schifano of *polypes ocellés* (ocellated), while the original spoke
of *soriani* polyps (thus evoking the striped coat of a tabby cat). This,
from a commonsensical point of view, means telling another story,
and to translate *soriano* with *ocellé* should be considered a crime in
every high school. But the translators had to make the following
interpretative decisions: (i) there is a 'deep' story (which could be
summarized by the macro-proposition 'Roberto swims toward the
coral reef and discovers for the first time in his life an unexpected
variety of colours'); (ii) this story must be respected because, by
telling it at the discursive level, (iii) the text clearly wants to

produce in the reader's mind the same chromatic impression – and such is the *intentio operis*, the *aesthetic aim* of that page; (iv) in order to produce its effect, the Italian discourse tells many 'surface' stories (Roberto sees such and such a coral, of such and such a colour); (v) these surface stories can be changed, even at the expense of close terminological correspondences, for the sake of the aesthetic goal.

The German translator found a more literal solution for my *polipi soriani*, by speaking of *Getigerte Polypen*. Probably that expression allowed him to maintain his own rhythm, while Weaver, Lozano, and Schifano felt disturbed by a more literal colour term. Notice that a little later I speak of 'tuberi tigrati' and when the translators used *striped tubers*, *tubercules tigrés*, and *raigones listados*, they could not use the same adjective for the polyps. Kroeber, having already called the polyps *getigerte*, was then obliged to change the form and colour of my tubers, speaking of *gelblich geflammte Knollen schwärzlichen Astwerks*, that is to say, roughly, of blackish branches shot through with yellowish protuberances.

One line below, I mention 'mentule albine con il glande d'amaranto.' *Mentula* is a Latin term for penis, and both Weaver and Kroeber translated it as *phalli*. Perhaps Schifano thought that the French term did not lend itself to the rhythm he had adopted, or to what he felt were the phonosymbolic values to be retained. Therefore he translates *mentula* as *olothuries*, a term that suggests a phallic form, knowing that the anatomical suggestion was reinforced immediately afterward by the mention of the glans.

In the first paragraph, I talk of 'corridoi di cretone,' using an archaic term for land rich in chalk. Weaver translates the term as *chalk*, and Kroeber avoids it by talking more generally of 'Schluchten und Schründen und Spalten,' thereby suggesting rocky fissures. For his part, Schifano seems to have taken *cretone* for *cretonne* (which is a fabric). But perhaps he wanted to keep the sound of the Italian word and, in a page full of similes and metaphors, an undersea corridor resembling a fabric is not out of place.

Another evident licence springs from my *avvinati*, a term that suggests a winelike colour, but which existed only in the Baroque period – and which at first sight could be taken for *avvinazzati* (drunk). Weaver overcomes the difficulty with *vinous*, which can mean both the colour of wine and drunk; Kroeber and Schifano opt for the alcoholic isotopy, and translate *weinselige* and *ivres*. I am not fully convinced that this is a simple misunderstanding: perhaps neither of the two translators had an equally precious word in their language, and so they preferred to shift the 'vinous' connotation of the colour to the apparently drunken movement of those multi-coloured fish. What I should like to emphasize here is that, when I read their translations in manuscript, I did not notice this change, a sign that the rhythm and the vivacity of the scene had struck me as having been rendered perfectly well.

So far, faced with the question regarding the extent to which translators can change the story, we can provide a first answer. Every sentence (or short sequence of sentences) of a discourse conveying a story can be summarized (or interpreted) by a micro-proposition. For instance, the few lines from chapter 57 of *Foucault's Pendulum* quoted above can be summarized as follows:

They are driving through the hills.
Diotallevi makes a literary remark about the landscape.

The micro-propositions can be embedded in larger macro-propositions. Thus, chapter 57 in its entirety could be summarized like this:

The characters drive through the hills of Piedmont.

They visit a curious castle in which many alchemical symbols are on
display.
There they encounter some occultists they had met before.

The whole novel could be summarized by a hyper-macro-propo-
sition that reads:

For fun, three friends invent a cosmic plot, and the story they imagined
comes true.

Given that stories are embedded in this way, to what extent are
translators entitled to change a surface story in order to preserve an
allegedly deep one?

It is clear that every single text allows for a different and individual solution. Common sense suggests that in *The Island of the
Day Before* translators can change 'Roberto saw a striped polyp' into
'Roberto saw an ocellated polyp,' but they certainly are not permit-
ted to change the global macro-proposition 'Roberto is shipwrecked
on an abandoned vessel just off an island that lies beyond the 180th
meridian.'

A first hypothesis is that one can change the literal meaning of
single sentences in order to preserve the meaning of the corresponding micro-propositions, but not the sense of major macro-
propositions. But what about many intermediate 'shallow' stories
(between the literal meaning of single sentences and the global
sense of an entire novel)? One could decide, for example, that if
character A tells a long stupid joke and if no literal translation can
render the stupidity of that joke, a translator is entitled to switch to
another joke, provided it remains clear that A tells silly jokes. It is
on the basis of interpretative decisions of this kind that translators
play the game of faithfulness.

TRANSLATING RHYTHM

During a seminar on translation, a colleague of mine gave the students the English version of *The Name of the Rose* (namely, the description of the church portal) and asked them to translate it into Italian (obviously threatening to compare their result with the original). Asked for some advice, I told the students that they were not to be disturbed by the idea that there was an original (in the same sense in which a translator should not be disturbed by the suspicion that there is a Perfect Language, a *reine Sprache*, somewhere in the skies). They had to consider the translation as if it were the original, and they had to decide what the purpose of that text was.

Literally speaking, it was the description of some monstrous figures sculpted on a church door that give young Adso a sort of vertigo. I told the students: where the English text says that there was 'a voluptuous woman, gnawed by foul toads, sucked by serpents ...,' the main problem was not to find the best Italian word for *gnawed* or necessarily to make those serpents suck. On the contrary, I asked them to read the entire page aloud, as if they were singing it, to listen to how the translator (to be considered as the author of that English text) had tried to set up a rhythm, a sort of rap, and to follow this rhythm. If, in order to preserve this rhythm, the serpents had not to suck but to bite, it did not matter; the effect would have been equally horrible.

I have a lot of experience working with the translators of my own texts, but very little as a translator of other people's texts. The most important of these forays into translation (in the sense that I did it after having spent decades reading and rereading a text I have always really loved) was the translation of Gérard de Nerval's *Sylvie*.[6] In the course of this task, I checked out about a dozen previous Italian translations, and four English translations. Every time I quote the French text, I shall provide a note with Sieburth's English translation, which in my view is the best.[7]

After having read this text a great many times, it was only on translating it that I became aware of a stylistic device that Nerval often uses. Without the reader's becoming aware of it (unless he reads the text out loud – as a translator must do if he or she wishes to discover the rhythm), in certain scenes with a powerful dream-like quality Nerval inserts metrical lines, sometimes complete Alexandrines, sometimes hemistichs, and sometimes hendeca-syllables. To make things easier for the reader, I have put the most evident of these lines in small capitals and separated the hemistichs with a slash.

In the second chapter (the dance on the lawn in front of the castle) there are at least sixteen metrical lines; for example, one hendecasyllable ('J'ÉTAIS LE SEUL GARÇON DANS CETTE RONDE'), Alexandrines (like 'JE NE PUS M'EMPÊCHER / DE LUI PRESSER LA MAIN'), and various hemistichs (like 'LA BELLE DEVAIT CHANTER' or 'LES LONGS ANNEAUX ROULÉS'). In addition there are internal rhymes (*placée, embrasser, baiser, m'empêcher* – all in the space of three lines). In the twelfth chapter, we find 'JE JUGEAIS QUE J'ÉTAIS / PERDU DANS SON ESPRIT.' Not to mention the splendid closing lines (chapter 14) 'TELLES SONT LES CHIMÈRES / QUI CHARMENT ET ÉGARENT / AU MATIN DE LA VIE,' followed by lines like 'TES OMBRAGES ET TES LACS / ET MÊME TON DÉSERT' or other hemistichs, such as 'COMME LES ÉCORCES D'UN FRUIT,' 'SA SAVEUR EST AMÈRE,' 'TOUT CELA EST BIEN CHANGÉ,' 'VOUS N'AVEZ RIEN GARDÉ,' 'QUELQUEFOIS J'AI BESOIN,' 'J'Y RELÈVE TRISTEMENT.'

Hence the decision to adhere to these rhymes as far as possible, even at the cost of forgoing a literal translation. For example, in chapter 14 I had first translated 'tes ombrages et tes lacs, et même ton désert' as 'le tue fronde ombrose e i tuoi laghi, e il tuo stesso deserto,' so as not to lose the double sense of *ombrages* (they are

leaves, and they give shade).[8] Then, in order to respect the Alexandrine, I gave up on shade, and chose 'LE TUE FRONDE E I TUOI
LAGHI / E IL TUO STESSO DESERTO.' Replacements do not always
work perfectly. Faced with 'NOS TAILLES ÉTAIENT PAREILLES' (when
the narrator is standing before the beauteous Adrienne in chapter 2,
where Sieburth translates, 'We were the same height'), I could not
manage to find a seven-syllable line that was as smooth, and I ran
aground on the shoals of a decasyllable that, if isolated, would
sound rather martial ('ERAVAMO DI PARI STATURA'). But even in this
case, in the flow of the discourse, I think that this scansion empha-
sizes the symmetry between the couple standing face to face.

In chapter 3, the evocation of Adrienne (half asleep) gives rise to
'FANTÔME ROSE ET BLOND / GLISSANT SUR L'HERBE VERTE, à demi
baignée de blanches vapeurs.' I managed to come up with 'FANTASMA
ROSA E BIONDO / LAMBENTE L'ERBA VERDE, / APPENA BAGNATA / DI
BIANCHI VAPORI' – and, as can be seen, after the two seven-syllable
lines I inserted a dodecasyllable.[9]

A little farther on we read: 'AIMER UNE RELIGIEUSE / SOUS LA
FORME D'UNE ACTRICE! ... / ET SI C'ÉTAIT LA MÊME? – Il y a de quoi
devenir fou! c'est un entrainement fatal où l'inconnu vous attire
COMME LE FEU FOLLET – fuyant SUR LES JONCS D'UNE EAU MORTE.' I
managed to respect the original rhythm, translating as 'Amare una
religiosa sotto le spoglie d'una attrice! ... E SE FOSSE LA STESSA? / C'È
DA PERDERNE IL SENNO! / È UN VORTICE FATALE / A CUI VI TRAE
L'IGNOTO, / FUOCO FATUO CHE FUGGE / SU GIUNCHI D'ACQUA
MORTA ...'[10]

In certain cases, we are faced with a dilemma: if we wish to save
something, we lose something else. See at the end of chapter 2,
when we read, as Adrienne is singing on the lawn, that 'la mélodie
se terminait à chaque stance PAR CES TRILLES CHEVROTANTS / QUE
FONT VALOIR SI BIEN les voix jeunes, quand elles imitent par un
frisson modulé la voix tremblantes des aïeules.'[11] There is a clear

cadence, reinforced farther on by a rhyme (the trills are *chevrotants* and the voice of the grandmothers is *tremblante*), and there is a play of alliterations that suggests the voices of the old ladies. Many Italian translators lose the cadence and the rhyme, and by way of alliteration they usually come up with 'tremuli' for *chevrotants* and 'tremolante' for *tremblante* (thus falling into an unpleasant repetition). I put my money on alliteration, saving two seven-syllable lines: 'La melodia terminava a ogni stanza CON QUEI TREMULI TRILLI a cui san dar rilievo LE VOCI ADOLESCENTI, quando imitano con un fremito modulato la voce trepida delle loro antenate.'

On other occasions, as usual, something has been recovered: again in chapter 2 we have 'J'ÉTAIS LE SEUL GARÇON DANS CETTE RONDE ... Où j'avais amené ma compagne toute jeune encore, SYLVIE, UNE PETITE FILLE,'[12] and in this way Sylvie makes her entrance borne along by a seven-syllable line, like a ballerina in her tutu. In Italian I didn't manage to bestow upon her the gift of such an entrance, although I did save the initial hendecasyllable, and so I had to content myself with anticipating it ('ERO IL SOLO RAGAZZO IN QUELLA RONDA, dove avevo condotto LA MIA COMPAGNA ANCORA GIOVINETTA, Sylvie, una fanciulla della frazione vicina ...'). As can be seen, sometimes I lost the Alexandrines and I introduced some hendecasyllables ('NON VEDEVO CHE LEI, SINO A QUEL PUNTO'); other times, knowing that I was going to lose a line shortly afterwards, I introduced it beforehand despite Nerval. In this way, I was unable to respect the Alexandrine 'JE NE PUS M'EMPÊCHER / DE LUI PRESSER LA MAIN' (which I translated with 'non potei trattenermi dallo stringerle la mano'),[13] but shortly before, where the text says only 'A peine avais-je remarqué, dans la ronde ou nous dansions, UNE BLONDE, GRANDE ET BELLE, / QU'ON APPELAIT ADRIENNE,' I introduce three hemistichs against the two in the original: 'AVEVO APPENA SCORTO, / NEL GIRO DELLA DANZA / UNA BIONDA, ALTA E BELLA, – che chiamavano Adriana.'[14]

To sum up, still in chapter 2, I managed to save all sixteen of Nerval's metrical lines, and I think I accomplished my goal – at least, provided they are not noticeable at first sight, just as they are not immediately apparent in the original.

As for the last chapter, here is the original and two translations that seek to preserve the rhythm:

Nerval: TELLES SONT LES CHIMÈRES / QUI CHARMENT ET ÉGARENT / AU MATIN DE LA VIE. J'ai essayé de les fixer sans beaucoup d'ordre, mais bien des cœurs me comprendront. Les illusions tombent l'une après l'autre, COMME LES ÉCORCES D'UN FRUIT, et le fruit, c'est l'expérience. SA SAVEUR EST AMÈRE; elle a pourtant quelque chose d'âcre qui fortifie, – qu'on me pardonne ce style vieilli.

Eco: TALI SON LE CHIMERE / CHE AMMALIANO E SCONVOLGONO / ALL'ALBA DELLA VITA. Ho cercato di fissarle senza badare all'ordine, ma molti cuori mi comprenderanno. Le illusioni cadono l'una dopo l'altra, COME SCORZE D'UN FRUTTO, / E IL FRUTTO È L'ESPERIENZA. / IL SUO SAPORE È AMARO; e tuttavia essa ha qualcosa di aspro che tonifica, – e mi si scusi questo stile antiquato.

Sieburth: Such are the chimeras THAT BEGUILE AND MISGUIDE US / IN THE MORNING OF LIFE. I have tried to set them down without much order, but many hearts will understand me. ILLUSIONS FALL AWAY one after another LIKE THE HUSKS OF A FRUIT, / AND THAT FRUIT IS EXPERI-ENCE. It is bitter to the taste, but there is fortitude to be found in gall – FORGIVE ME MY OLD FASHIONED turns of phrase.

At this point, we can discard a lot of puzzling definitions of translation that have recourse to similarity of meaning or to other circular arguments. Instead of speaking of equivalence of meaning, we can speak of *functional equivalence*: a good translation must generate the same effect aimed at by the original (cf. Mason 1998, Schäffffner 1998).

Obviously this means that translators have to make an interpretative hypothesis about the effect programmed by the original text. Many hypotheses can be made about the same text, so that the decision about the focus of the translation becomes *negotiable*.

HOW NOT TO GET MORE AND HOW TO ACCEPT LESS

There are translations that splendidly enrich the target language and that, in cases that many consider to be felicitous, manage to say more (in other words, are richer in suggestion) than the originals. But, in fact, these translations are usually valuable in themselves as original works of art, and not as versions of a source text. A translation that manages to 'say more' might be an excellent piece of work in itself, but it is not a good translation.

I shall give a very limited example, which concerns a possible 'enhancement,' a very marginal one, but one that allows me to explain what I mean.

In the course of my translation of *Sylvie*, I had to make a lexical decision regarding the fact that at the beginning, when she is still a naïve country craftswoman, a *cage de fauvettes* appears in Sylvie's room. Later, when Sylvie has all but become a city dweller (and the narrator feels that by then she is lost to him, lost forever), her room, by then furnished in a more sophisticated manner, contains a cage of canaries.

If we look in an Italian-French dictionary for the meaning of *fauvettes*, we find that they are called 'silvie.' These are cases in which the translator is tempted to go beyond the intentions of the original text. Just think, 'le silvie di Silvia,' or Sylvie's *silvie*! The stuff of a deconstructionist's dreams! Unfortunately, Nerval spoke

French and could not have been aware of this play on words. Translating sometimes means rebelling against one's own language, when it introduces effects of sense that were not intended in the original. If the translator were to insert that play on words, he or she would be betraying the intentions of the source text.

In fact, all the Italian translators opted for *capinere* (blackcaps, and the *capinera* is a *Sylvia atricapilla*). Sieburth chose *linnets* (which would be *grisets* in French and therefore *Carduelis cannabina)*, but it doesn't make much difference: in any case, we are dealing with wild birds, which are captured in the countryside, and are opposed to canaries insofar as they are not domesticated birds.

It has been said that Nerval uses a limited vocabulary. Certain terms are repeated on several occasions – the peasants' complexion is always *halée*, visions are pink and powder blue or pink and blonde, blue or bluish shades appear eight times, there are nine pink hues, while the adjective *vague* appears five times and the word *bouquet* nine times. But before we talk about lexical poverty, we ought to reflect upon the play of correspondences (in Baudelaire's sense of the word) that the text sets up between different images. Therefore the rule ought to be never to enhance the author's vocabulary, even when tempted to do so. But the translator is unfortunately obliged to use variations on certain occasions.

Let us take a look at the term *bouquet*. I said that it appears nine times, and it is clear why Nerval uses it in such abundance. The theme of a floral offering runs through the whole story: flowers are offered to Isis, to Adrienne, to Sylvie, to Aurélie, to the aunt, and just for good measure at a certain point even a *bouquet de pins* makes its appearance. These flowers are passed from hand to hand, like a sceptre, in a sort of symbolic relay race, and it is only right that the author uses the same word to emphasize the recurrence of the motif.

Unfortunately, *bouquet* translates into Italian as 'mazzo,' and it's not the same thing. This is so because *bouquet* conveys a connotation of subtle aromas, and calls up flowers and leaves, while a *mazzo* may also be made of nettles, keys, socks, or rags. Therefore *bouquet* is a delicate word while *mazzo* is not, as it suggests crude terms like *mazza* (cudgel), *mazzata* (blow with a cudgel), or *ammazzamento* (killing, pole-axing); it is cacophonic and sounds about as delicate as a whiplash.

I envy Sieburth, who was able to use *bouquet* seven times out of nine, but Webster's recognizes the term as an English word. True, Italian dictionaries now do the same, but in common usage *bouquet* applies to the bouquet of a wine, and if it is applied to a bunch of flowers it sounds like a Gallicism. I feel that in a translation from French it is necessary to avoid using Gallicisms, just as it is necessary to avoid Anglicisms in a translation from English. I was therefore obliged to vary the term at every occurrence, choosing from *serti*, *fasci*, and *mazzolini* according to circumstances. It was some consolation to think that, while I had lost a word, I had not lost the image of the floral offering, and the recurring motif had been preserved. Nonetheless, I realize that I betrayed Nerval's style, which is still style even if it contains repetitions.

In any case, the translator must not waste too much time trying to avoid gaining something, because when translating, one is not so much likely to gain as to lose something.

The last chapter of *Sylvie* is called 'Dernier feuillet.' It is a sort of farewell, a melancholy seal set at the end of the work. Nerval was a bibliophile (a fact which emerges from many of his texts), and he used a technical term: the English for *feuillet* is *leaf*, a page of a book (consisting of two sides, *recto* and *verso*). The 'dernier feuillet' usually contains the colophon, indicating when the book was printed and by whom, and in old books at times also containing words of farewell, or a religious invocation. Sieburth translates this correctly as 'Last leaf,' while another English translation gives 'Last pages,' thus losing the allusion to old books. The technical term in Italian for *feuillet* is *carta*, but 'ultima carta' risked introducing an extraneous connotation because in Italian the expression 'giocare l'ultima carta' means the same as its equivalent in English, to play one's last card, that is, to make a last-ditch attempt to remedy a situation. This connotation would have betrayed the sense of the original as the narrator here is doing nothing of the sort; on the contrary, he has resigned himself to his fate and takes melancholy leave of his own past. I could have translated *feuillet* as *ultimo folio*, falling back on a Latin expression, used in a technical sense in catalogues of antique books (for example, all countries use the term *in folio* to indicate the format of a book). But Nerval did not want to introduce this technicality, which would have been (and still would be) incomprehensible to the average reader. Therefore I decided to translate, slightly inaccurately, 'ultimo foglio.' As a matter of fact, the *carta* of a book in Italian is also called the *foglio*, but *foglio* is a less technical word than *carta*. And so I realize I have lost an important allusion.

But, in other cases, losses can be *compensated* for.

COMPENSATING FOR LOSSES

Still with regard to Sylvie, we are told that both the houses of her village, Loisy, and her aunt's house, which the two protagonists visit at Othys, are *chaumières*. *Chaumière* is a fine word that does not exist in Italian. Italian translators opt variously for *capanna*, *casupola*, *casetta*, or *piccola baita*. Sieburth gives *cottage*.

Now, the French term expresses at least five properties: a *chaumière* is (i) a peasant's house, (ii) small, (iii) usually made of stone, (iv) with a thatched roof, (v) humble. It's impossible to say it in Italian in only one word, especially if one has to add, as happens in chapter 6, that the aunt's *petite chaumière* was 'en pierres de grès inégales.' This is not a *capanna*, which in Italian suggests a wooden structure. It is not a *casetta* because it has a thatched roof (while the Italian *casetta* has a tiled roof, and is not necessarily a poor dwelling), but neither is it a *baita*, which is a crude construction found in the mountains, a temporary refuge. I feel that not even *cottage* is entirely appropriate, because this might mean a small bungalow. The fact is that in many French villages in that period the houses of the country folk were like that, but this does not mean they were either bungalows or wretched shacks. It is therefore necessary to forgo some of the properties (because in trying to make them all explicit there is a risk of supplying a dictionary definition, thereby losing the rhythm), and to salvage only those relevant to the context. Regarding the houses of Loisy, I thought it better to give up the thatched roofs in order to make it clear that they were 'casupole in pietra' (small stone houses). I have lost something, and into the bargain I have already had to use three words in place of one. As for the aunt's house, the text says it was made of *grès*, which translates as *arenaria* in Italian (and ought to be *sandstone* in English), but the term conjures up regularly cut stones (I always think of the charming sandstone house where Nero Wolfe usually lives, a house that all Rex Stout's readers know well). It could be said, as indeed the text says, that the house is made of irregular sandstone blocks, but in Italian such a specification obscures the fact that it had a thatched roof. In order to give contemporary Italian readers a visual impression of the house, I had to drop the (all things considered, irrelevant) detail that the house was made of sandstone, and I limited myself to saying that it was a stone house. By adding that it had a thatched roof, I think I allowed people to imagine that those stone walls constituted an *opus incertum*. The subsequent specification (the walls were covered with trellises upon which there climbed wild hops and honeysuckle) ought to convey the idea that the house, although humble, was no hovel. Compare the original, my translation, and Sieburth's version:

> *Nerval*: La tante de Sylvie habitait une petite chaumière bâtie en pierres de grès inégales que revêtaient des treillages de houblon et de vigne vierge.

> *Eco*: La zia di Sylvie abitava in una casetta di pietra dai tetti di stoppia, ingraticciata di luppolo e di vite selvatica.

> *Sieburth*: Sylvie's aunt lived in a small cottage built of uneven granite fieldstones and covered with trellises of hop and honey suckle.

In chapter 13 we are told that the lover of Aurélie (the actress beloved of the protagonist, who is opposed to the image of the unattainable Sylvie) makes his exit, leaving the field free, because he has enlisted in the *spahis*. His is also a definitive exit, because the *spahis* were colonial troops, and therefore the nuisance was headed overseas. But how many non-French readers (and perhaps even modern French readers) are able to appreciate this subtlety? Many Italian translators talk faithfully of *spahis*, as does Sieburth, who is, however, obliged to add a note: 'Algerian cavalry units in the French army.' One Italian translator talks of 'cavalleria coloniale' and lets it be understood that the suitor has gone far away. I followed this choice, in part, without losing altogether the *foreignizing* effect of *spahis*, and opted for 'si era arruolato oltremare negli *spahis*' (he had enlisted overseas in the *spahis*). By adding a single adverb, I avoided the footnote, which is always a sign of weakness on the part of a translator.

WHEN THE TEXT HAS US SEE THINGS

As I said apropos of *The Island of the Day Before*, verbal texts often bring into play processes of hypotyposis; in other words, they lead the language to 'stage' something that the reader is virtually led to *see.*

For example, in translating Nerval, one cannot avoid noticing that he (man of the theatre as he was) describes many scenes as if it were a question of creating them for the stage, especially as far as lighting is concerned. The actress with whom the narrator is in love appears in chapter 1 bathed in the glow of the footlights and then in that of a lantern, but theatrical lighting techniques are already in play during the first dance on the lawn, where the last rays of sunlight filter in through the foliage of the trees that serve as the wings; and as Adrienne is singing the moonlight falls on her alone (and she exits from what today we would call the 'spotlight' with the grace of an actress taking leave of her public). In chapter 4, in the 'journey to Cythera' (which is apart from anything else the verbal representation of a visual representation, because it is inspired by a painting by Watteau), the scene is once more illuminated from above by the vermilion rays of the sunset. In chapter 7, when the narrator joins the dance at Loisy, we are in the presence of a masterpiece of theatre direction in which the bottoms of the linden trees are gradually enveloped in shadow while their tops are tinged with a bluish colour, until, in this struggle between artificial lighting and coming day, the scene is slowly pervaded by the pale light of morning.

These are all cases in which a careful translator, following what we might describe as the 'stage directions' supplied by the original text, can obtain the same effects. But there are cases in which, in order to show something, Nerval uses terms that must have been familiar to readers of his day, but may be obscure for modern readers, and even for modern French readers themselves. It is as if a contemporary text, which says, 'He switched on the computer in the dark room, and stood as if hypnotized,' were read by a reader of one hundred years ago who has never seen a computer. This reader would not have the immediate impression of a luminous screen coming to life in the darkness, nor could she or he understand why this created a hypnotic effect.

I should now like to make a detailed analysis of the chapter in which Sylvie and the narrator visit her old aunt at Othys, because it seems to be a textbook case. In this section there is a kind of enchanted return to the preceding century: the aunt allows her niece to go into her bedroom and rummage among the mementos of her youth, at the time of her marriage to Sylvie's uncle (by that time dead), and we have as it were an epiphany of a late eighteenth-century pastoral-genteel kitsch. But in order to realize what Sylvie and her friend discover, we need to understand some archaic terms, connected with the fashions of those far-off days (which Nerval's contemporaries certainly still understood).

At this point, the translator ought to behave as if he or she were a director who means to transpose the story into film. But the translator cannot use either images or detailed specifications, and must respect the rhythm of the story, because descriptive *longueurs* would be fatal.

What does it mean to say, in a portrait, that the aunt as a young girl appears 'élancée dans son corsage ouvert à échelle de rubans'? The various Italian translators chose from among 'corpetto aperto sul davanti a nastri incrociati'; 'corpetto dai nastri a zig-zag'; 'corpetto, aperto coi nastri incrociati sul davanti'; 'camicetta aperta a scala di nastri'; 'corpetto aperto a scala di nastri'; 'corsetto aperto sotto la scala dei nastri'; 'corsetto aperto a nastri scalati'; 'corpetto aperto in volantini di nastri'; 'corsetto aperto a scala di nastri'; 'corpetto aperto ed allacciato dai nastri incrociati sul davanti' – and Sieburth offers 'slender in her open bodice laced with ribbons.' The garment was certainly not a blouse and perhaps not even bodice is entirely satisfactory; there is no indication as to how open it is in front, and few people know what an 'échelle de rubans' is. Now, a 'corsage à échelle de rubans' is a bodice with a generous scoop neck that goes at least as far as the first swelling of the bosom and is fastened by a series of knots of decreasing size to form a wasp waist. An example is to be seen in Boucher's portrait of Madame de Pompadour. This corset is certainly coquettish and elegant – it gives a generous view of the bosom and tapers down to form a seductively narrow waist – and this is what counts. And therefore I preferred to talk of a 'corsetto dalla vasta scollatura serrato a vespa da grandi nastri,' or a 'corset with a deep scoop neck fastened by large ribbons to form a wasp waist' (and that the ribbons are in scale ought to be suggested by the fact that the corset fastening gets progressively narrower toward the waist).

One of the points that puzzled translators is the 'grande robe en taffetas flambé, qui criait du froissement de ses plis,' which the two youngsters find in a drawer. Sieburth talks of 'a flowing gown of shot silk whose every fold rustled at her touch.' First of all, what does *flambé* mean? It certainly should not be translated, as many Italian translators translated it, as 'squillante,' 'luccicante,' 'color bruciato,' or even 'sciupato' (as one translator did, seduced by a familiar use of the term *flambé*, meaning someone who has ruined himself or herself). A clue is given by the fact that the French word *flammé*, which Italian dictionaries all translate as 'fiammato,' is a technical term meaning a weave made using many skeins of different colours so that one hue blends into another to create a streaky, flamelike effect. If this is the case, some are right to define it as an iridescent taffeta, and this seems to be Sieburth's solution, given that (when said of a fabric) *shot* also means 'woven with threads of different colours so as to appear iridescent' (Webster). Unfortunately, the directress of the Musée de la Mode in Paris, who had at first opted instinctively for 'cangiante,' then checked on the matter and told me that *flambé* means 'orné de fleurs dont les teintes se fondent,' specifying that the expression would have been used for a damask.

A damasked fabric leads one to think of the skirt worn by Madame de Pompadour in Boucher's portrait of her, with the *corsage à échelle de rubans*. But if a great lady of the court had a damask skirt, Sylvie's aunt had to be content with one in taffeta, albeit in taffeta *flambé*. Any translation that hinted at a fabric with damasked highlights would suggest more than it should. What to do? Especially because this taffeta did not merely rustle, as Sieburth translates, but (as Nerval says) *criait*. In their attempts to render this 'cry,' the other Italian translators (in a crescendo of decibels) offer variously 'si sentiva leggermente frusciare,' 'frusciava con le sue pieghe,' 'frusciava da ogni piega,' 'era tutto frusciante nelle sue pieghe,' 'faceva con le pieghe un gran fruscio,' 'strideva dalle pieghe gualcite,' 'strideva, frusciante, dalle sue pieghe,' 'faceva un gran chiasso con il fruscio delle sue pieghe,' and 'rumoreggiava allegramente nello scuotersi delle sue pieghe.' In some translations, this fabric whispers, and in others it makes too much noise. Evidently this 'cry' is not only auditory, but visual too.

Now we cannot propose to provide the reader with an encyclopedia entry on the textiles industry. Here the matter is the thrilling effect on the two youngsters both of the iridescence, or at least the multiple nuances of the fabric, and the freshness (I would dare say, but do not say, 'crackling' quality) of its folds. I decided to take that taffeta as *flammé* rather than *flambé*, and using the corresponding Italian term, which on the one hand seems archaic (or mysterious at any rate) and, on the other, metaphorical, transfer the 'cry' to the visual and auditory connotations of flames. In the end, I saved the overall iridescent effect. The result: 'un taffettà fiammato, che cangiava colore a ogni fruscio delle sue pieghe.' Perhaps the fabric was something different, but I trust that the reader may 'see' and 'touch' it as Sylvie and her friend do, and that the appeal of that garment emerges clearly, in opposition to the limp and decidedly non-majestic item that Sylvie suddenly removes. In fact, 'déjà Sylvie avait dégrafé sa robe d'indienne et la lassait tomber à ses pieds.' The dictionary authorizes us to translate this printed cotton fabric as 'Indian.' Many Italian translators talk of an Indian dress or outfit, but my fear is that in this way Sylvie may strike the reader as being as lexically challenged as a cartoon red Indian. Some Italian translators talk of 'il vestitino di tela stampata' or 'la sua veste di tela indiana.' The explanatory paraphrase is correct, but it is so at the expense of the rhythm. Sylvie strips it off suddenly, and we must respect the rapidity of her graceful and innocently provocative gesture. Sieburth translates it, rightly in my view, as 'Sylvie had already undone her calico dress and let it slip to her feet.' I chose the term *cotonina*, which means a cheap printed cotton, and I translated as 'aveva slacciato il suo abito di cotonina sfilandolo sino ai piedi.'

After putting on her aunt's dress, Sylvie complains of her 'manches plates,' and everyone translates this as 'maniche lisce – o piatte,' but in this case it is not clear why the narrator remarks by contrast how those 'sabots garnis de dentelles découvraient admirablement ses bras nus' or, as Sieburth says, 'the lace-trimmed puffs showed off her bare arms.' In short, are these sleeves plain or fancy? Faced with the problems posed by the text, Sieburth does without the plain sleeves and has Sylvie say only: 'These sleeves are ridiculous.'

The fact is that the 'manches plates' (also called 'manches à sabots' or 'sabots') were short flared lace-trimmed sleeves popular in the eighteenth century (some histories of dress talk of the Watteau style), but they did not have puffed shoulders as prescribed by nineteenth-century fashion. Therefore Sylvie found that they drooped over her shoulders too much, because they did not have the 'puff,' as it was known. In order to help the reader understand how the sleeves were, and why Sylvie was complaining, I ignore the literal meaning of the text and have the girl say: 'Oh, come cadono male, le spalle senza sbuffo!' (Oh, how sleeves without a puff hang badly!). Immediately after, instead of trying to translate 'sabots garnis de dentelles,' I say that 'la ˒ ːta merlettatura svasata di quelle maniche metteva mirabilmente in mostra le sue braccia nude' (the short flared lacework of those sleeves displayed her bare arms admirably). Readers should at once 'see' those Watteau-style sleeves and understand that Sylvie finds the outfit unfashionable – and perhaps smile at her concept of modernity. Another way of suggesting times long gone by.

I won't go on to describe how I translated other terms that Nerval thought would help us see other objects found in the drawer. In all these cases, I always avoided a literal translation and, without losing the rhythm by describing these objects in too much detail, used an adjective to suggest their appearance. I shall finish with a pair of stockings, which Sylvie puts on in the end, and which are described as 'des bas de soie rose tendre à coins verts.' Almost all the translators took these for pink stockings with green toes and heels, and I even saw an illustrated edition of the story in which the (twentieth-century) artist depicted them that way.

But Sylvie had said that she was looking for (and had found) 'bas brodés,' and therefore embroidered stockings made of silk and not patchwork woollen stockings. In the Pléiade edition of Nerval's works there is a note (evidently indispensable for modern French readers too) according to which *coins* are 'ornements en pointe à la partie inferieure des bas,' and I think that the intention is to allude to certain lateral decorations, from the ankle to mid-calf, occasionally embroidered with a fishbone pattern, known in Italian as *freccia* or *baghetta*. The Musée de la Mode informed me that 'les coins sont des ornements – souvent des fils tirés come les jours des draps – à la cheville, parfois agrementés de fils de couleurs differentes.' It seems to me that Sieburth had understood something of the kind, given that he talks of 'pale pink stockings with green figure-work about the ankles.' In order to avoid showing off all I had learned about 'coins verts,' and to ward off any suspicion that I might be in competition with some embroidery magazine, I thought it appropriate to talk simply of 'calze di un color rosa tenero, trapunte di verde alla caviglia.' I think this ought to suffice to give the reader a glimpse of that rather touching horror.

COMPENSATION THROUGH REWRITING

There are cases in which the loss involved in adhering strictly to the text is quite irreparable. In such cases, if we wish to obtain the same effect that the text was designed to provide, we have to *rewrite*. I shall be saying more on rewriting as a free form of translation later on, but for the moment I shall offer only a few examples of *moderate rewriting*.

In my novel *The Name of the Rose* there is a character, Salvatore, who speaks a language made up of fragments of a variety of languages. Naturally the introduction into the Italian text of foreign terms produced an effect of defamiliarization, but if a character said 'Ich aime spaghetti' and an English translator rendered this multilingual expression as 'I like noodles,' the 'Babel' effect would be lost. Here therefore is how three translators managed to rewrite, in their respective languages and cultures, the speech of my character:

'Penitenziagite! Vide quando draco venturus est a rodegarla l'anima tua! La mortz est super nos! Prega che vene lo papa santo a liberar nos a malo de todas le peccata! Ah ah, ve piase ista negromanzia de Domini Nostri Iesu Christi! Et anco jois m'es dols e plazer m'es dolors ... Cave el diabolo! Semper m'aguaita in qualche canto per adentarme le

carcagna. Ma Salvatore non est insipiens! Bonum monasterium, et aqui
se magna et se priega dominum nostrum. Et el resto valet un figo seco.
Et amen. No?'

'Penitenziagite! Watch out for the draco who cometh in futurum to
gnaw your anima! Death is super nos! Pray the Santo Pater come to
liberar nos a malo and all our sin! Ha ha, you like this negromanzia
de Domini Nostri Jesu Christi! Et anco jois m'es dols e plazer m'es
dolors ... Cave el diabolo! Semper lying in wait for me in some
angulum to snap at my heels. But Salvatore is not stupidus! Bonum
monasterium, and aquí refectorium and pray to dominum nostrum.
And the resto is not worth merda. Amen. No?' (*Weaver*)

'Penitenziagite! Voye quand dracon venturus est pour la ronger ton
âme! La mortz est super nos! Prie que vient le pape saint pour libérer
nos a malo de todas les péchés! Ah ah, vous plait ista nécromancie
de Domini Nostri Iesu Christi! Et anco jois m'es dols e plazer m'es
dolors ... Cave el diabolo! Semper il me guette en quelque coin pour
me planter les dents dans les talons. Mais Salvatore non est insipiens!
Bonum monasterium, et aqui on baffre et on prie dominum nostrum.
Et el reste valet une queue de cerise. Et amen. No?' (*Schifano*)

'Penitenziagite! Siehe, draco venturus est am Fressen anima tua! La
mortz est super nos! Prego, daß Vater unser komm, a liberar nos
vom Übel de todas le peccata. Ah, ah, hihhi, Euch gfallt wohl ista
negromanzia de Domini Nostri Jesu Christi! Et anco jois m'es dols e
piazer m'es dolors ... Cave el diabolo! Semper m'aguaita, immer
piekster und stichter, el diabolo, per adentarme le carcagna. Aber
Salvatore non est insipiens, no no, Salvatore weiß Bescheid. Et aqui
bonum monasterium, hier lebstu gut, se tu priega dominum nostrum.
Et el resto valet un figo secco. Amen. Oder?' (Kroeber)

In *Foucault's Pendulum*, I introduce a character, Pierre, who speaks a very 'Frenchified' Italian. No problem for the other translators, who merely had to think of how someone would speak with a French vocabulary and accent in their language, but the French translator found himself faced with some serious problems. He could have chosen to introduce a character whose vocabulary and accent were (let's say) German or Spanish, but he realized that my character referred to situations typical of *fin de siècle* French occultism. The translator therefore decided to stress, not the fact that my character was French, but that he was a caricature, and he made him speak in a manner that suggested Provençal origins.

In *The Island of the Day Before*, Father Caspar is a German priest who not only talks with a German accent, but also transposes directly into Italian the syntactical structures typical of the German tongue, again with caricatural effects. Here is a passage in Italian, followed by the French and English versions created by the translators, whose goal was to reproduce in their languages some errors typical of a German speaker:

'Oh mein Gott, il Signore mi perdona che il Suo Santissimo Nome invano ho pronunziato. In primis, dopo che Salomone il Tempio costruito aveva, aveva fatto una grosse flotte, come dice il Libro dei Re, e questa flotte arriva all'Isola di Ophír, da dove gli riportano (come dici tu?) ... quadringenti und viginti ...'

'Quattrocentoventi.'

'Quattrocentoventi talenti d'oro, una molto grossa ricchezza: la Bibbia dice molto poco per dire tantissimo, come dire pars pro toto. E nessuna landa vicino a Israele aveva una tanto grosse ricchezza, quod significat che quella flotta all'ultimo confine del mondo era arrivata. Qui.'

'Ach mein Gott, the Lord forgive I take His most Holy Name in vain.

In primis, after Solomon the Temple had constructed, he made a great
fleet, as the Book of Kings says, and this fleet arrives at the Island of
Ophir, from where they bring him – how do you say? – quadrigenti
und viginti ...'
    'Four hundred twenty.'
    'Four hundred twenty talents of gold, a very big richness: the Bible
says very little to say very much, as if pars pro toto. And no land near
Israel had such big riches, quod significat that the fleet to ultimate edge
of the world had gone. Here.' (*Weaver*)

'Oh mein Gott, le Seigneur me pardonne pour ce que Son Très Saint
Nom en vain j'ai prononcé. In primis, après que Salomon le Temple
construit avait, il avait fait une grosse flotte, comme dit le Livre des
Rois, et cette flotte arrive à l'Ile d'Ophir, d'où on lui rapporte (Comment dis-toi?) ... quadringenti und viginti ...'
    'Quatre cent vingt.'
    'Quatre cent vingt talents d'or, une beaucoup grosse richesse: la Bible
dit beaucoup peu pour dire tant et tant, comme dire pars pro toto. Et
aucune lande près d'Israël avait une aussi tant grosse richesse, quod
significat que cette flotte aux derniers confins du monde était arrivée.
Ici.' (*Schifano*)

This time it was the German translator's turn to find himself in
serious difficulties. He got round the problems by deciding that
Father Caspar's most important characteristic was not so much the
fact he was German, as a German of the seventeenth century, and
he had the character speak in a kind of Baroque German. The effect
of defamiliarization is the same, and Father Caspar emerges as
equally bizarre. Note, however, that it was not possible to render
another comic trait of Father Caspar, who, when he has to say
quattrocentoventi (four hundred twenty) in Italian, hesitates. A German would say *fier hundert zwanzig*, and therefore there would be

no problem, but Father Caspar is evidently thinking of other cases in which in order to say, let's say, *ventuno* (twenty one), which in German would be *ein und zwanzig*, he has translated as *uno e venti* (one and twenty), and therefore he hesitates, opting to go for the Latin. Obviously, in a German translation, this wordplay would be quite insipid, and the translator was obliged to eliminate a question and an answer and to weld two of Caspar's dialogues into one:

> 'O mein Gott, der Herr im Himmel vergebe mir, daß ich Sein' Allerheyligsten Namen unnütz im Munde gefüret. Doch zum Ersten: Nachdem König Salomo seinen Tempel erbauet, hatte er auch eine große Flotte gebaut, wie berichtet im Buche der Könige, und diese Flotte ist zur Insel Ophir gelangt, von wo sie ihm vierhundertundzwanzig Talente Goldes gebracht, was ein sehr gewaltiger Reichthum ist: die Biblia sagt sehr Weniges, um sehr Vieles zu sagen, wie wann man saget *pars pro* toto. Und kein Land in Israels Nachbarschafft hatte solch grossen Reichthum, was bedeutet, daß diese Flotte muß angelanget gewesen seyn am Ultimo Confinio Mundi. Hier.' (*Kroeber*)

In all these examples, the translators have certainly achieved the same effect as the Italian text had evidently produced. Nevertheless, the very fact that I am obliged to talk of rewriting reveals that we are on the borders of the notion of translation. When is a translation no longer a translation but something else? This is the topic we shall have to tackle in the second part of these lectures.

NOTES

1 In this example, I invited the translator to disregard the literal sense of my text in order to preserve what I considered to be the 'deep' one. It may be objected that in such a case I was providing an allegedly 'correct' interpretation of my

own text, thus betraying my conviction that authors should not provide interpretations of their own works. As a matter of fact, even authors can act as good readers of their own texts, able to detect the *intentio operis* (see Eco 1979), that is, what the text actually says, independently of the author's intentions. Usually I invite my translators to pay attention to a certain passage which, according to the general context of the novel, should suggest something beyond its literal sense. As for the dialogue cited above, the translator was obviously the first to realize that a literal translation could not work, and my contribution consisted not in providing an 'authorized' interpretation but in encouraging an alternative solution – as if I were a co-translator.

2 According to Quine, the indeterminacy of translation arises from the fact that rival systems of analytical hypotheses can produce different (but equally legitimated) translations of the same sentence. 'Just as we meaningfully speak of the truth of a sentence only within the terms of some theory or conceptual scheme ... so on the whole we may meaningfully speak of interlinguistic synonymy only within the terms of some particular system of analytical hypotheses' (1960, ii, 16). If Quine's position only concerned the comparison between two languages, the picture of what we are doing when we translate would be incomplete. As a matter of fact, we bring into play not only two languages but also two cultures. In doing so – that is, by increasing the number of variables – we are not increasing but rather reducing the rate of indeterminacy and are helped in trying to reach a reasonable interpretative decision. To follow Quine's famous example, if the jungle linguist has difficulties in deciding whether *gavagai* means rabbit or rabbit stage, this is because the linguist has no previous information on the native culture – in other words, he or she does not know how the natives categorize things, parts of things, and events involving things. If successful, a system of analytical hypotheses should produce not only a linguistic manual but a whole anthropological handbook.

3 I understand that these solutions were rather risky. The readers of different languages were induced to believe that my three Italian characters had a sort of native competence in non-Italian literature. But in this case (and only in this case), the risk was an acceptable one. My characters worked in a publishing house and had frequently shown their erudition in comparative literature.

4 When an Italian writer or politician is mentioned in the British press, the Italian *signore* is used. To Italians, reading 'Signor Moravia said that ...' or 'Signor Prodi will do such and such' not only seems comic but often offensive.

In Italian, the connotation is that the person whom one is attacking is not very well known. When in the course of a polemic it is said – of a public figure – 'Signor Rossi thinks that ...' the intended tone is insulting. The use of the surname alone ('Rossi thinks that ...') is far more polite than putting *signor* before the name.

5 A propos of the influence of translations on the target language, let me stress the fact that, after the dubbing of many American movies in which priests were called *padre*, gradually many Italians abandoned the traditional *don* and switched to the American usage.

6 Just how important this text has been for me as a scholar and a writer has already been explained in the first chapter of *Six Walks in the Fictional Woods*. My translation, with comments, appeared as Nerval, *Sylvie* (Turin: Einaudi, 1999).

7 Nerval, *Sylvie*, trans. Richard Sieburth (London: Penguin, 1995).

8 Sieburth: 'What are to me now, your lakes, your shadowy groves, your desert?'

9 Sieburth: 'A PHANTOM FAIR AND ROSY / GLIDING OVER THE GREEN GRASS / HALF BATHED IN WHITE MIST.' I think that both Sieburth and I have 'given' Nerval an extra verse, evidently to make up for those cases in which we did not manage to follow his rhythm.

10 Sieburth: 'TO BE IN LOVE WITH A NUN / IN THE GUISE OF AN ACTRESS! ... and what if they were one and the same! It is enough to drive one mad – the fatal lure of the unknown drawing one ever onward LIKE A WILL O' THE WISP / FLITTING OVER THE RUSHES of a stagnant pool.'

11 Sieburth: 'At the end of every stanza, the melody trailed off into one of those wavering trills which young voices know how to produce so effectively whenever they modulate their tremolo in imitation of the quavering voices of their grandmothers.'

12 Sieburth: 'I was the only boy in the round, and I had brought along my little friend, Sylvie, a girl from the neighbouring village ...'

13 Sieburth does the same: 'I could not resist GIVING HER HAND A SQUEEZE.'

14 Sieburth: 'I had barely noticed the tall, beautiful fair-haired girl by the name of Adrienne.'

Translation and Interpretation

In his essay on the linguistic aspects of translation, Jakobson (1959) suggested that there are three types of translation: *intralinguistic*, *interlinguistic*, and *intersemiotic*. Interlinguistic translation occurs when a text is translated from one language to another; in other words, when we have 'an interpretation of verbal signs by means of signs of some other language' (which is translation proper). Intersemiotic translation (and in this lay the most innovative feature of his proposal) occurs when we have 'an interpretation of verbal signs by means of signs of non-verbal sign systems,' and therefore when a novel is 'translated' into a film, for example, or a fairy tale into a ballet. Note that Jakobson also proposed to call this form of translation 'transmutation,' and the term should give us food for thought – but we shall come back to this point. However, the first kind of translation Jakobson mentioned was intralinguistic translation, also called 'rewording,' which he defined as 'an interpretation of verbal signs by means of other signs of the same language.'

Jakobson's distinction did not take into account certain phenomena that require discussion. First of all, just as *rewording* exists within a language itself, so there are also forms of *rewording* (but this would be a metaphor) within other semiotic systems, as, for example, when we change the key of a musical composition. Secondly, in talking of transmutation, Jakobson was thinking of a version of a verbal text in another semiotic system (in Jakobson 1960, the examples offered are the translation of *Wuthering Heights* into film, of a medieval legend into a fresco, of Mallarmé's *Après midi d'un faune* into a ballet, and even of the *Odyssey* into a comic strip); but he does not deal with other cases of transmutation between systems other than verbal language, like, for example, the ballet version of Debussy's *Après midi*, the interpretation of 'Pictures in an Exhibition' by means of a musical composition by Mussorgsky, or even the version of a painting in words (*ekphrasis*).

But the most important problem is another. In order to define the three types of translation, Jakobson uses the word *interpretation* three times, and it could not be otherwise for a linguist who, while belonging to the structuralist tradition, was the first to discover the fecundity of Peircean concepts. His definition of the three types of translation thus left us with some ambiguity. If all three types of translation are interpretations, did Jakobson not mean that the three types of translation are three types of interpretation, and that therefore translation is a species of the genus *interpretation*? This seems the most obvious solution, and the fact that he insisted on the term *translation* could have been due to the fact that he wrote down his reflections for a collection of essays called *On Translation* (Brower 1959), in which his aim was to distinguish between various types of translation, implicitly taking for granted that they were all forms of interpretation. But, on the grounds of Jakobson's proposal, many people decided that he was suggesting a diagram of this type:

intralingual
rewording

Translation   **interlingual**
translation proper

intersemiotic
transmutation

Since, as we shall see, the category of *rewording* covers an immense variety of types of interpretation, at this point it would be easy to succumb to the temptation to identify the totality of semiosis with a continuous process of translation; in other words, to identify the concept of translation with that of interpretation.

Jakobson, like many others after him, was fascinated by the fact that on several occasions Peirce had turned to the idea of translation in order to define the notion of interpretation. That Peirce speaks on many occasions of interpretation as translation is undeniable. It suffices to cite his *Collected Papers* (*CP*) 4.127, in a context in which he specifically reiterates his central idea that the meaning of a sign is expressed by its interpretation through another sign (in the broadest sense in which Peirce employs the term *sign*, with the result that the meaning of the sign *jealousy* could be interpreted by Shakespeare's *Othello* as a whole). Here Peirce is emphasizing for the hundredth time that the meaning of an expression is (or can only be rendered explicit by) 'a second assertion which all that follows from the first assertion equally follows, and vice-versa.'

The central point of his reasoning is this: in agreement with the pragmatic maxim, the principle of interpretance establishes that every more or less elusive 'equivalence' between two expressions can only be given by the identity of consequences that they imply or make implicit. To make his point more clearly, Peirce, in the same context, asserts that *meaning*, in its primary sense, is a 'translation of a sign into another system of signs.'

Peirce's vocabulary is notoriously protean and often impressionistic, and it is easy to notice that in this, as in other contexts, he uses *translation* in a figurative sense: not like a metaphor, but *pars pro toto* (in the sense that he assumes 'translation' as a synecdoche for 'interpretation').[1] In this context, Peirce is arguing against certain logicians ('those people') with regard to the meaning of the expression 'immediate neighbourhood' used in the definition of the speed of a particle. We are not concerned with the nature of the debate, but with Peirce's questioning of the idea that *immediate neighbourhood* is a simple conventional expression that is not otherwise definable. According to Peirce, it should be *interpreted* (perhaps by means of an icon, as in fact he does in this same paragraph), and only in this way would we know its 'meaning.' He wants to explain what *to interpret* means, and therefore it is as if he were developing, in an elliptical fashion, the following argument:

(i)   Meaning results when one expression is replaced by another expression from which follow all the illative consequences that follow from the first.

(ii) If you don't understand what I mean, think of what happens in a process whose laboriousness is obvious to anyone, and that is the (ideal) translation of a sentence from one language to another language, in which it is presumed or demanded that all the illative consequences from the expression in the target language follow all the illative consequences that follow from the expression in the source language.

(iii) Translation from language to language is the most obvious example of how we try to say the same thing using different sign systems.

(iv) This capacity, and this interpretative laboriousness, do not concern only translation from language to language, but also all attempts to make the meaning of an expression clear.

Even though Peirce never worked on translation from language to language *ex professo*, he nonetheless did not fail to notice the specificity of this phenomenon with respect to the many other modes of interpretation, and the fact that he knew how to make distinctions is demonstrated by Gorlée (1994: 168, in particular). But Peirce's synecdoche fascinated Jakobson (1977: 1029), who asserted enthusiastically: 'One of the most felicitous, brilliant ideas which general linguistics and semiotics gained from the American thinker is his definition of meaning as "the translation of a sign into another system of signs" (4.127). How many fruitless discussions about mentalism and anti-mentalism would be avoided if one approached the notion of meaning in terms of translation ... The problem of translation is indeed fundamental in Peirce's views and can and must be utilized systematically.'

Jakobson was simply saying that the notion of interpretation as translation from sign to sign allows us to get round the diatribe about where meaning lies, in the mind or in behaviour, and he does not say that interpreting and translating are always the same operation, but that it is useful to tackle the notion of meaning in terms of translation (I would like to add: *as if* it were a translation). In explaining Jakobson's position, in a long article on his contribution to semiotics, I wrote: 'Jakobson demonstrates that to interpret a semiotic item means "to translate" it into another item (maybe an entire discourse) and that this translation is always creatively enriching the first item ...' (Eco 1977: 53). As you can see, I put 'to translate' between inverted commas, to indicate that this was a figurative expression. My reading might be debatable, but I would like to point out that I submitted my essay to Jakobson before publishing it and that he had discussed various points, certainly not in an attempt to force conclusions upon me that were different from those I had reached (that was not his style), but in order to specify, to make things scrupulously clear, and to suggest references to other writings of his that confirmed my reading. On that occasion, no objections were made to my inverted commas. If Jakobson had thought them misleading, insofar as I was quoting him nearly verbatim, he would have pointed out to me that he had intended to use 'to translate' in a technical sense.

If anything, what is debatable in the above quotation from Jakobson is the conclusion that the reference to translation, being fundamental to Peirce's thinking, would have to be used 'systematically.' But here, too, it seems to me that Jakobson wanted to say that it is always necessary to bear that aspect of the problem of meaning in mind, not that it is necessary to establish an absolute equivalence between translation and interpretation.[2]

In spite of this, as I have already pointed out, the idea that the entire activity of interpretation is to be thought of as translation continued to absorb those who came after. See Steiner (1975) in a chapter called 'Understanding as Translation.' He reiterates that the object of his study is interlinguistic translation, and that translation in the strict sense of the term is only a particular case of the communicational relationship that every successful linguistic act describes within a given language. But he holds that this model of interpretative deciphering makes all the phenomena of linguistic understanding clear. Further on (1975, IV, 3), he admits that a theory of interlinguistic translation can take two paths: either it is the way to designate the operating model of *all* meaningful exchanges (including Jakobson's intersemiotic translation or transmutation), or it is a subsection of that model. Steiner concludes that the first path is more instructive, but, after making his preference clear, he is shrewd enough to admit that the choice can only depend on an underlying theory of language. As we shall see further on in this essay, I start evidently from another theory of language, and I do so explicitly, maintaining that my choice is more faithful to that of Peirce and – despite appearances – to that of Jakobson.

Paolo Fabbri (1998: 115–16) seems to share Steiner's position. He says that, 'if we read Peirce carefully, we notice that according to this author the sign, in relation to the other sign, is not a simple reference; according to Peirce, in fact, the meaning of a sign is the sign into which it must be translated,' and this is naturally beyond dispute. Fabbri admits immediately that perhaps this is a metaphor, but proposes to 'take it seriously.' Therefore, after a reference to Lotman, he asserts positively that '*the act of translation is the first act of signification*, and that things signify thanks to an act of translation internal to them.' Fabbri evidently means that the translation principle is the basic motivating force of semiosis, and therefore that every interpretation is in the first place a translation (which is, in fact, a way of taking the so-called Peircean metaphor seriously).

To take a metaphor seriously means extracting all possible suggestions from it, not transforming the vehicle of the metaphor into a technical term. And it is precisely by trying to make the metaphor work at full speed that Fabbri, on the following page, is happily forced to limit its capacity. We shall have more to say about his views later, but it should suffice to say that he is aware (as many people are not) that there is a limit to translation, when we are confronted with 'diversity in the purport of expression.'[3] Having identified this limit, we are forced to say that, *at least in one case*, there are forms of interpretation that are not wholly comparable to translation between natural languages.

I shall now try to show that the universe of interpretations is vaster than that of translation proper. My dwelling on this point is not merely a lexical question. If it were merely a question of words, and if we meant always to use *translation* as a synonym for *interpretation*, all we would need do is agree on the matter. The fact is that the variety of semiosis gives rise to phenomena whose difference is of the maximum importance for the semiologist. For the 'layman' it should be sufficient to be aware that human beings communicate, understand and misunderstand one another, and that sometimes things go well and sometimes badly. But the whole purpose of studying semiotics is to understand these differences and to see how much they count in semiosic processes. It may be asserted, for example, that in the operations Jakobson calls transmutation (turning the *Divine Comedy* into a comic strip, let's say) it is possible to do a better job of rendering the deep significance of the *Divine Comedy* than by making a clumsy translation of it into Swahili. This is another problem to be dealt with later, but first of all it should be understood that it is one thing to make a summary of the *Divine*

Comedy in Italian, and another to translate it into Swahili, and another again to make it into a comic strip.

TRANSLATIO

The term *translatio* first appeared in the sense of 'change,' even of address, 'transport,' banking operation, botanical graft, and metaphor. Only in Seneca does it appear as a turning from one language into another. Likewise *traducere* meant 'to lead beyond.' The passage from transporting something from one place to another to translating from one language to another seems to be the result of an error by Leonardo Bruni, who had interpreted Aulus Gellius (*Noctes* I, 18) incorrectly: 'Vocabulum graecum vetus traductum in linguam romanam,' where this means that the Greek word had been transported or transplanted into Latin. In any event, *tradurre* in its modern sense was common currency in the fifteenth century, and it supplanted (in Italian and French, at least) *translatare* (English, on the contrary, transported – in the ancient sense of *traducere* – the Latin *translatare* into its lexicon, thus coining *to translate*; see Folena 1991).[4]

Many dictionaries give, among the several meanings of 'to translate,' also the action of transforming data or instructions from one form or from one given alphabet into another form or alphabet, without loss of information. Such information will certainly include references to systems of *transcription* like the Morse code, to signalling systems using small naval flags, and even to the so-called genetic code. But it is clear that, on a linguistic level, the model of transcription could at most be applied to phrase books for tourists that establish, in a rather perfunctory way, that *dog* = *chien* and that *coffee* = *café*, without even realizing that, in the last case, equivalence holds for the drink but not for the place where the drink is served, which is *coffeehouse* or *cafeteria* in English, *café* in French, and *caffè* in Italian. It is clear that in the processes of translation proper there are margins of decision according to the context. These are, however, absent in transcription processes, in which there is no freedom of choice.

REWORDING AS INTERPRETATION

But let us get back to intralinguistic translation. Jakobson's term *rewording* leads one to think that this is a matter of saying something using other words from one's own language. Now phenomena of this sort include straight, and often illusory, synonymy, such as the *father* = *dad* definition, which can be very schematic (like *cat* = 'mammalian feline') or extremely wordy (such as an encyclopedia entry for cat), as well as paraphrase and summary, but also scholia, comments, and popularization (expressing something difficult with simple words), all the way to the most complex inferences.

In other words, so-called intralinguistic translation includes most of the phenomena of interpretation defined by Peirce, and so the meaning of an expression can be interpreted by another expression, and the meaning of that second expression in its turn by another still, and so on potentially *ad infinitum*, except for the cases in which the chain of interpretants ends up as the final logical interpretant, that is, the formation of a *habit*, which leads us to act on reality, and this habit in its own turn is an interpretation of the original expression. Since, moreover, a verbal expression can also be interpreted by a visual expression, a gesture, or a sequence of sounds (a performance of Beethoven's *Fifth* in its entirety would always be an interpretation of the expression 'Fifth symphony in C minor'), in this case ought we simply to speak of intersemiotic translation, as when the same *Fifth* was translated into a ballet? I think not, insofar as the use of non-verbal interpretants to interpret a verbal expression is much more internal to linguistic praxis, in the sense that we are continuously holding up objects to make clear the meaning of a word, or emphasizing deictics like *here* or *there* by means of gestures. All of which demonstrates the variety of types of interpretation and the scant usefulness of defining them all as translation.

In this semiosic series of interpretants, every interpretation, according to Peirce, says something more about the expression interpreted. At first sight, it seems that it can also say something less, as if a complete description of the form and the behaviour of a cat were interpreted by the 'mammalian feline' definition. But, in effect, the definition – no matter how telegraphic – also tells us where in the animal taxonomy to put the animal that has already been abundantly described, and therefore it says something more. Furthermore, the process of interpretation can render explicit that which was implicit, or even absent, in the original expression, given that a complete interpretation of the word *cat* would also include the information that cats were worshipped by the Egyptians, or seen as diabolical animals in the Middle Ages.

If the concept of interpretation is to be assumed in its widest sense (and its semiotic fecundity makes this advisable), it is clear that translation, at least in the sense of interlinguistic translation, is only a very limited type of interpretation. Even if only from an intuitive standpoint, nobody would think that a ten-page version of *David Copperfield* written in Italian was a translation. At most, one might consider it a summary. Anyone who summarized the *Divine Comedy* in English by saying that it is 'a powerful and fascinating representation of the destiny of human souls in Hell, Purgatory, and Paradise' would certainly be providing a succinct interpretation of the entire poem, perhaps maintaining that only in such a way could its deep nature be expressed, but, once again, it would be pure (and not very perspicuous) rhetorical licence to call it a translation.

DEFINITION VERSUS TRANSLATION

Likewise, some people think that expressions like "mammalian feline" or "domestic animal that miaows" elucidate the meaning of the word *cat*: if one said that those expressions were translations of *cat*, there would be a total identification of the expressed meaning and translation. It would not be merely a question of words. Let us take the first quatrain of Baudelaire's 'Les chats':

(i)

Les amoureux fervents et les savants austères

Aiment également, dans leur mûre saison,

Les chats puissants et doux, orgueil de la maison,

Qui comme eux sont frileux et comme eux sédentaires.

An English translation gives:[5]

(ii)

Fervent lovers and austere scholars

Love equally, in their ripe season,

Powerful and gentle cats, the pride of the house,

Who like them are sensitive to cold and like them sedentary.

This is a literal translation without any particular pretensions to equalling the source text, but it could be said that anyone starting from (ii) in order to reconstruct (i), would obtain something semantically (if not aesthetically) fairly analogous to Baudelaire's text. In fact, when I asked Altavista's automatic translation service to turn the English text into French, I got:

(iii)
Les amoureux ardants et les disciples austères
Aiment également, dans leur saison mûre,
Les chats puissants et doux, la fierté de la maison,
Qui comme eux sont sensibles au froid et les aiment sédentaires.

Next experiment!

It must be admitted that from the semantic point of view we have recovered much of the original text. The only real error, in the fourth line, occurs when the adverb *like* is mistaken for a verb. Except for this 'slip,' (ii) was no better: it preserved neither rhyme nor metre, while this mechanical *rewording* at least retains the first Alexandrine (perfectly) and two rhymes, thus showing that (i) had a poetic function.

Now let us assume, following Webster's *New Universal Unabridged Dictionary* (if *rewording* is thought to be a form of translation), that:

lover: a person who loves
scholar: a learned person
ripe: fully grown or developed
season: any one of the four arbitrary periods into which the year is divided
cat: species of carnivorous quadruped of the genus Felis
sedentary: fixed to one spot

Let us replace the terms of the first English version with their dictionary definitions:

(iv)
The fervent persons who love and austere learned persons

Love equally, in any one of their fully grown or developed four arbi-
trary periods into which the year is divided,
A powerful and gentle species of carnivorous quadrupeds of the genus
Felis, the pride of the house,
Who like them are sensitive to cold and like them fixed to one spot.

On handing (iv) back to Altavista we got:

(v)
Les personnes ardantes qui aiment et les personnes instruites austères
Aiment également, dans toutes de leur entièrement développé ou
développé quatre périodes arbitraires où l'année est divisée,
Une espèce puissante et douce de quadrupèdes carnivores du genre
Felis, la fierté de la maison,
Qui comme eux sont sensibles au froid et les aiment fixés à une tache.

It has become a joke. But this joke has been made possible by
having identified translation and interpretation through definition,
and that is by having rigorously (mechanically) respected the (evidently absurd) principle that definition is a form of translation of
that which is defined. I should now like to quote the Italian
translation by Mario Bonfantini:[6]

(vi)
I fedeli d'amore, e gli austeri sapienti
Prediligon, negli anni che li fanno indolenti,
I gatti forti e miti, onor dei focolari
Come lor freddolosi, come lor sedentari.

The translator has decided to vary the (literal) semantic values;
for example, with the debatable reference to 'fedeli d'amore' (which
opens up a list of connotations extraneous to the text).[7] He has

rendered the age of maturity with the years of indolence (not an entirely arbitrary decision), because indolence belongs to the same associative field as the sedentary state; he has (legitimately) rendered *doux* with 'miti' (docile) and *maison* with 'focolari' (hearth). The success of the translation is due to the fact that the translator has managed to turn two alternating rhymes (*abba*) into two rhyming couplets (*aabb*), and above all he has respected the Alexandrine by using double seven-syllable lines.[8]

In other words, the translator has decided that, over and beyond the literal sense of the French expressions, the effect or main aim to be respected was the poetic one, and that was the card he put all his money on. Debatable as a paraphrase or exact *rewording*, this translation constitutes an excellent interpretation of the intentions of the text.

This leads us to conclude that translation is a species of the *genus* interpretation, governed by certain principles proper to translation.

BUONGIORNO

Let us suppose that someone asks us to explain the sense of the expression *buongiorno* (and it would be the same with *bonjour* and, within certain limits, with *guten Tag* and *good day*). We might say that, literally, it could be a description of a fine or joyful day, but that, according to current conventions, when pronounced holophrastically it is a greeting whose function is first and foremost a phatic one; while in the second place, it represents the hope that the person being greeted will have a day devoid of worries and full of satisfaction, even though the sincerity of the wish is much less important than the attempt to make a show of courtesy and of the absence of aggressiveness (except for particular suprasegmental versions, in which the greeting, pronounced in a clipped manner through clenched teeth, is intended to indicate hostility). The phatic function is so important that *buongiorno* could be replaced (when people are on first-name terms) with *come va* (how's it going?), without any risk of compromising the interaction.

This entire paraphrase of the term *buongiorno* would be a case of good interpretation, but not of 'translation,' and the proof of this is that if, having interpreted in English the meaning of *buongiorno*, on meeting someone I were to say, (a) 'In accordance with the phatic use of language and for reasons of courtesy, I wish you an easy and happy day,' I should at the very least be thought of as bizarre. And the same thing would happen if I said in French, (b) 'Selon la fonction de l'utilisation phatique du langage et par politesse je vous souhaite une journée heureuse et agréable.' Of course, (b) would be generally accepted as a fair translation of (a), but both (a) and (b) would be understood as interpretations (in the sense of *rewordings*), and not translations, of *buongiorno*.

What happens when, instead, I decide to translate *buongiorno* as *bonjour* or *good day*? We have already excluded the notion that there is a passage involving a Perfect Language or some type of 'Mentalese' in the process of translating from language to language. Therefore, and remaining faithful to the Peircean notion of interpretation, on hearing the Italian expression *buongiorno*, I move on to interpret its content and deem as adequate interpretants those expressions that, even if they enhance the content of the expression interpreted, could be adequately interpreted by it in their turn (for example, if [a] is an adequate interpretation of the meaning of *buongiorno*, it could be interpreted in its turn by the expression *buongiorno*). In doing this, however, I do not merely keep to the semantic value but also to the pragmatic value of the expression. If I were to stick only to semantic values, then I could translate *buongiorno* with *good day*, which is a current expression, but perhaps less refined; moreover, I would have to know that *buongiorno* is usually translated as 'good morning' or 'good afternoon' according to the (temporal) circumstances of the utterance. If I have to translate into French a *buongiorno* uttered at the beginning of an interaction, I will not translate it as *bonne journée* (which would be semantically equivalent) because the French say *bonjour* at the beginning of the interaction and *bonne journée* (which is, moreover, a rather unrefined and informal expression) only when taking their leave. If I had to translate *bonne journée* into English, still in the light of current linguistic usage, I would translate it as 'have a nice day' or even 'take care' (just as I would translate it into Italian as *stia bene!* but I would not translate this Italian expression with the more literal, but ridiculous, 'may you stay well').

Attempts to make these translations adequate depend on the effect (in this case, social) required, and the interpretation must pursue this effect. Why would it be inadvisable to translate *bonne journée* with 'I hope you will have good and enjoyable experiences for the rest of the day'? Why would it be inviting criticism to translate 'attento allo scalino' as 'I advise you to pay attention to the step whose presence may perhaps have escaped your notice' and not as 'mind the step'? From the point of view of interpretation there would be no objection, and it could be said that the effect we wanted to achieve is the same. The point is that a basic ingredient of any greeting, like conventional warnings, is *brevity*. A good translation of a greeting or a warning must retain the swiftness with which it is proffered.

THE SUBSTANCE OF THE EXPRESSION

Now this type of brevity is not just a matter of linguistic considerations. Let us take another look at Hjelmslev's distinctions between form, substance, and purport, both from the point of view of expression and from that of content.

Many misunderstandings can spring from the fact (and I must

number myself among those responsible for this) that in order to explain Hjelmslev's concepts, and therefore for reasons of didactic clarity, his doctrine has been synthesized with a diagram of this kind:

	continuum or purport
Content	substance
	form
	form
Expression	substance
	continuum or purport

This diagram certainly shows the difference between Hjelmslev's various concepts, but it leaves us with the impression that it is a homogeneous classification, while it is not. For Hjelmslev, given the same sonic continuum, two languages A and B segment it differently, producing two different forms of the expression. Once the form of the expression has shaped the continuum, which, prior to that moment was an amorphous possibility, the continuum is formed, and it is that form that interests linguists. In terms of systems, the linguist considers only relations between forms.

Substance is not a system phenomenon. It appears only when, by exploiting the possibilities provided by a given linguistic system, one *physically* produces a *text*. The substance of an expression is produced, materially, only when a communication process begins, that is, when sounds are emitted according to the rules of a given language.

The same thing happens with content. A given culture carves content-forms (sheep *vs.* goat, horse *vs.* mare, and so on) out of the content continuum, but the substance of the content is realized as the *sense* that a given element of the form of the content assumes in a given co-text. Only in the framework of an uttered text may we establish that, in that co-text and in a given circumstance of utterance, the expression *horse* refers to that form of the content that opposes it to other animals.

Thus we should consider a different diagram, namely:

SYSTEM	TEXT
	content substance: sense of a given text
content form	sense of a given term in that co-text
expression form	grammatical and stylistic form of the discourse
	expression substance

The substance of the expression also changes in *rewording* operations, like definition or paraphrase, because in saying that *cat* should be interpreted as *Felis Catus*, two substances of the expression have been produced. The two substances are different because, so to speak, they have a different material consistency, or a different 'weight' (the second one takes up more space when it is written; and, when spoken, it produces sonic vibrations that are different from the first, and it leaves a different imprint on a magnetic tape). It is essential, however, if we are to have adequate *rewording*, that with this change of substance we intend to express the same form of the content (*Felis Catus* would have to define with greater exactitude the difference, on a level of the form of content, between a cat and a lion, *Felis Leo*). In ideal enunciatory circumstances, we could say that the two expressive substances 'there is a cat on the mat' and 'there is a Felis Catus on the mat' would also have to express the same substance of the content, to the point that, still in ideal circumstances, the reader ought not to think that the change of substance was important. Instead, 'there is a cat on the mat' and 'il y a un chat sur le tapis' characterize the same substance of the content, but through two forms of expression (one in the English-language system and one in the French-language system), and the difference in the substances assumes a certain importance (lesser for a bilingual person, greater for someone wrestling with the first principles of French).

Let us try to sum up and consider the following expressions:

(i) Go home.

(ii) Please go back to where you habitually dwell.

(iii) Torna a casa.

In (i) two different English speakers (who, for example, have two different regional accents) use the same form of expression to bring into play two different expressive substances, whose variations are not relevant, so as to express the same substance of the content. Jakobson would have said that the two phonations convey an 'equivalent message.' The substance of the expression only becomes relevant when it acquires ironic connotations. For example, Paolo Fabbri and I like to amuse guests, in the wee small hours, with a certain recital. I read Leopardi's 'A Silvia' with a strong Piedmontese accent, and he reads D'Annunzio's 'La pioggia nel pineto' with a Romagna accent. The effect is comic, in spite of the seriousness of the texts recited. This comic effect is due to a change in the substance of the expression, but this change is reflected in the way in which the substance of the content is identified, and so inevitably people laugh not only at us, but also at Silvia and Hermione.

In (ii), within the same form of the expression, a substance of the expression that is considerably different from (i) is produced, in the attempt to interpret differently the same substance of the content (equivalent message). However, the use of language also contemplates attention to stylistic values, and there is no doubt that (ii) reveals an excess of precision that could assume ironic connotations. Therefore, in suitable circumstances, the difference in the substance of the expression (which transforms a command or a very curt invitation into a materially longer locution, and relates to the form of the message produced, not the form of the linguistic system, which remains the same) can act as a clue pointing to a pragmatic difference.

In (iii) we have an attempt to render the same substance of the content of (i) ('equivalent message') using a different form of the expression, with a consequent change of substance of the expression, relevant this time, although not decisive (for a bilingual person, the two commands obtain the same effect without any attention being paid to the change of substance, which at most can connote only the ethnic origin of the person making the injunction). A change of form and substance of the expression becomes decisive in particular circumstances; for example, when *go home* is yelled by non-English-speaking demonstrators, who with that injunction wish to convey a specific message to English-speakers who have settled in their territory, while the same thing would hold if racist Europeans pronounced the Arabic translation of (i) during an anti-immigration demonstration.

According to Hjelmslev (1943: 47), in the passage between two languages, a translation is considered adequate when, given two different forms of the expression, it is possible to identify the same continuum or 'purport' of the content: for example, *I do not know*, *je ne sais pas* and *jeg véd det ikke*, which manifest three different forms of expression, have a common content purport. Hjelmslev's idea of the purport of the content is notoriously controversial. See Eco (1997: 1) for a reconsideration of the problem. For the purposes of this present discourse, however, it seems sufficient to me to observe that in the three expressions cited here attempts are made to retain (in the difference in form and substance of the expression) the same *substance* of the content. Very often, in the passage from language to language, attempts are made also to conserve the same form of the content.

Let us return to (ii), a typical operation of *rewording*. As long as we identify the same substance of the content, we are extremely indulgent as far as the substance of the expression is concerned. To interpret *buongiorno* as an 'expression with a phatic function, with which we hope that the interlocutor has a day devoid of worries and full of satisfaction – even though the sincerity of the wish is less important than the intention to manifest courtesy and an absence of aggressiveness' is wholly satisfactory from the point of view of *rewording* because the 'physical weight' of the substance of the expression is not pertinent. This is why a treatise in ten volumes on cats can be understood as a satisfactory interpretation, of encyclopedic size, of the word *cat*.

As we said, in (iii), with translation into another language, the substance begins to acquire importance. Of course, when the sign on trains 'it is dangerous to lean out' is translated as 'il est interdit de se pencher au dehors,' such is the need to convey the information in an adequate fashion (so as to create the effect of a warning and an imposition) that a compromise has to be reached regarding the remarkable differences within the substance of the expression. But we have seen in the case of greetings that brevity is pertinent, and this already allows us to glimpse the fact that in a translation issues regarding the substance of the expression are often important. In Bonfantini's translation of Baudelaire, questions of the substance of the expression acquire such importance that we can accept a remarkable degree of licence on the content level. The Italian *focolare* (hearth) stands for *maison* only by metonymy. In reality, its connotations have more to do with the intimacy and warmth of a traditional country home, and it evokes the presence of

a fireplace or a stove, while *maison* circumscribes a broader semantic space, and Baudelaire's text could also suggest that the 'savants
austères,' thin blooded as they are, live in a big cold house whose
rooms are full of bookcases.

But the translator was interested first and foremost in preserving
the metre and the rhyme, which are not linguistic, but rhetorical
and stylistic, phenomena. Thus we can understand why the brevity
of greetings is important. Greetings belong to a conventional style
that, insofar as it is highly regulated, has something liturgical about
it. Now conventional and liturgical formulas in the proper sense
(like *Ite missa est*) border very closely on poetic language, and must
respect stylistic norms.

STYLISTIC VALUES AND EXPRESSIVE SUBSTANCE

Rhetoric recognizes figures of content (like metaphor, synonym, or
oxymoron) in which the substance of the expression is not pertinent ('une forte faiblesse' translates 'a strong weakness' very well
with different sounds); but it becomes important in the majority of
figures of expression, like paronomasia, assonance, alliteration, or
anagram (as we have already seen, 'j'aime bien Ike' is not an
adequate translation of 'I like Ike'). The expressive substance likewise becomes fundamental with regard to phonosymbolic issues,
and to discursive rhythm in general.

As for the metric values, the length of vowels and syllables is a
system phenomenon, like the tonic accent (which in the Italian
lexical system, for example, establishes differences of meaning); but
taking a sequence of sounds of different length and articulating
them in a syntagm in accordance with the laws of quantitative
metre, or in accordance with the number of syllables and their
accent, is a phenomenon of the organization of the discursive

process and these solutions (even though they also depend on particular metrical and stylistic rules) are perceptible only as phenomena of the substance of the expression. Rhyme (and the rhyme scheme) is likewise perceptible as the substance of the expression, even if it exploits elements already supplied by the lexical system.

Now see what happens with a poem like Poe's 'The Raven,' where, after a series of verses that end with *nothing more* and *evermore* (rhyming with *door, floor, before, implore, explore,* and *Lenore*), the raven, and the lover, begin to repeat obsessively, *nevermore*. For example:

> 'Ghastly grim and ancient Raven wandering from the night shore –
> Tell me what thy lordly name is on the Night's Plutonian shore!'
> Quoth the Raven 'Nevermore.'
>
> ...
>
> Ever yet was blessed with seeing bird above his chamber door –
> Bird or beast upon the sculptured bust above his chamber door,
> With such name as 'Nevermore.'
>
> ...
>
> Till I scarcely more than muttered 'Other friends have flown before –
> On the morrow he will leave me, as my Hopes have flown before.'
> Then the bird said 'Nevermore.'

In his 'Philosophy of Composition,' Poe stressed the evocative value of that reiterated *nevermore* (and the other expressions that rhyme with it), which constitute as it were the poetic hinge of the entire text, the key to the *effect* that he wished to create in the reader: 'I decided to vary, therefore, to increase the effect, by sticking, in general, to the monotony of the sound, while I continuously modified that of thought ... Naturally, the facility of the variation would have been in proportion to the brevity of the phrase. This induced me immediately to conclude that a single word would have made the best refrain ... The refrain had to end each verse. That such a conclusion, in order to have force, had to be sonorous and to sustain an extended effort of the voice, there was no doubt, and so these considerations unavoidably induced me to adopt the long *o*, that is the most sonorous vowel, and the *r*, the consonant that prolongs the vowels longest.' Hence the choice of *nevermore*, which Poe presents as obligatory. Obligatory or otherwise as it may have been at the moment of creation, it should be so for every translation, and this constitutes a dramatic and practically insurmountable obstacle, which shows that the problem is not semantic, but phonosymbolic, and everything depends on the substance of the expression.

In his French translation, Gabriel Mourey[9] keeps some rhymes or assonances before the two closing lines of every verse but, when he comes to the decisive moment, he forgoes any attempt at phonosymbolic effects:

'Corbeau fantômal, sombre et vieux, errant loin du rivage de la Nuit –
Dis-moi quel est ton nom seigneural sur le rivage Plutonien de la Nuit!'
Fit le Corbeau: 'Jamais plus.'
...
Car nous ne pouvons empêcher de convenir qu'aucun être humain
     vivant n'eût jamais la bénédiction de voir un oiseau sur la porte de sa
     chambre –
un oiseau ou une bête sur un buste sculpté au-dessus de la porte de sa
     chambre,
avec un nom tel que 'Jamais plus.'
...
jusqu'à ce que je murmurai à peine, 'D'autre amis se sont envolées déjà –
demain il me quittera, comme mes Espérances se sont envolées déjà.'
Alors l'oiseau dit: 'Jamais plus.'

In this translation, the abrupt sound of *plus* undermines part of the effect the text was intended to generate, the 'extended effort of the voice.'

The Portuguese translation by Fernando Pessoa[10] retains internal rhymes and assonances in the course of the various verses, but it too gives up on the rhyming effect of *nevermore*. Whereas, thanks to the employment of the *u*, the French *Jamais plus* preserves a phono-symbolic effect of gloom, the Portuguese loses it by entrusting it to other, clearer vowels. But perhaps it has rediscovered a way to render the extended effort of the voice:

> Ó velho Corvo emigrado lá das trevas infernaes!
> Dize-me qual o teu nome lá nas trevas infernaes.
> Disse o Corvo: 'Nunca mais.'
>
> ...
>
> que uma ave tenha tido pousada nos seus humbraes,
> ave ou bicho sobre o busto que ha por sobre seus humbraes,
> com o nome 'Nunca mais.'
>
> ...
>
> perdido, murmurai lento, 'Amigo, sonhos – mortaes
> todos ... todos já se foram. Amanhã também te vaes.'
> Disse o Corvo, 'Nunca mais.'

While in a translation of a practical-informative nature we can assume that *nunca mais* or *jamais plus* are reasonable synonyms for *nevermore*, in the case of Poe's poem we cannot, because the substance of the expression is pertinentized. Which is what was said in Eco (1975, 3.7.4) when it was stated that in texts with a poetic function (even when not just linguistic texts) the continuum of expression is further segmented.

In Eliot's 'The Love Song of J. Alfred Prufrock' there is the famous verse

> In the room the women come and go
> Talking of Michelangelo.

It is clear that, as throughout the poem for that matter, the text plays on rhymes or assonances, internal ones too, and sometimes obtains, as in this case, ironical effects (created by the Anglicized pronunciation of the Italian name). In order to avoid grotesque solutions, a translator may forgo both metre and assonance. This is what Luigi Berti and Roberto Sanesi did:[11]

> Nella stanza le donne vanno e vengono
> Parlando di Michelangelo.

In the French translation,[12] Pierre Leyris attempts to maintain an effect of rhyme by changing the meaning of the source expression:

> Dans la pièce les femmes vont et viennient
> En parlant des maîtres de Sienne.

We get the impression that, while the rhyme has been saved, we have lost the humour of the original assonance, based on that one / ö /. As we can see, the most demanding thing is the play on the substances.

EXPRESSIVE SUBSTANCE AND AESTHETIC EFFECT

This relevance of the substance is central to discourse with a poetic function and in every art, where what counts is not only that we can see, in a picture, for example, a mouth or an eye on a face, but that we can appraise the line, the brush stroke, and often the clot of matter with which they are realized (and, in fact, we say *substantiated*).

In communications with a practical purpose, the presence of the expressive substance is purely functional: it serves to strike the senses, and thence we set off to interpret the content. If I were to ask someone where Prufrock is, and that person told me he is in the room in which some women are talking about Michelangelo, the pronunciation of the name, and the fact that in the course of the phrase there is an assonance with *go*, would be inessential: I would forget the substance of the expression (and the form, too), taking care to identify the right room, perhaps discarding another in which a raven is croaking *nevermore* before some austere sages.

Instead, confronted with a discourse whose function is poetic, I certainly grasp both the denoted and the connoted content (those ladies are probably bluestockings), but after having done that, I go back to the substance of the expression, and I delight in the relation between that same substance and the content.

We have been talking about translation as a strategy that aims to produce, in a different language, the same effect as the source discourse, and poetic discourse is said to aim at producing an aesthetic effect. But Wittgenstein (1966) wondered what would happen if, once the effect that a minuet produces on listeners were identified, we could invent a serum that, duly injected, supplied the nerve endings of the brain with the same stimuli as produced by the minuet. He observed that it would not be the same thing because it is not the effect but *that* minuet that counts (see Rustico 1999). The aesthetic effect is not a physical or an emotional response, but an invitation to see how a particular physical or emotional response is caused by a particular form in a sort of continuous 'shuttling' back and forth between effect and cause. Aesthetic appreciation is not just a matter of the effect one experiences, but also involves an appreciation of the textual strategy that produces it. This appreciation also involves the stylistic strategies brought into play on the level of the substance of expression. This is another way of saying, as Jakobson does, that poetic language is self-reflexive.

The translation of a poem ought to permit the same 'shuttling' between expression and content. The difficulty of working on the substance of expression ensures – and this is a very old argument – that poetry is harder to translate than every other kind of text. In poetry, as I have said elsewhere (Eco 1985: 253), it is a series of constrictions on the level of expression that determines the content, and not vice-versa, as happens in discourses with a referential function.

This is why, in the translation of poetry, one often aims at *rewriting*, as if accepting the challenge of the original text so as to recreate it in another form and another substance (trying to keep faith, not with the letter, but with the 'guiding spirit' of the text, whose identification obviously depends on the translator's critical interpretation). But I shall have more to say about rewriting later, and for now I should like to consider an anomalous, although not infrequent, case in the typology of interpretation.

CHANGE OF CONTINUUM

To get back to Poe's 'The Raven,' a translator could permit himself a good deal of licence in order to render the effect that the source text seems to wish to create. For example, in order to retain the rhythm or the rhyme, there would be no harm in changing the 'pallid bust of Pallas' into that of some other divinity, provided that the bust remained white. With the bust, Poe wanted to create a contrast between the blackness of the raven and the whiteness of the statue, but the bust of Pallas Athena, Poe points out in 'The

Philosophy of Composition,' 'was chosen, primarily, as the one most suited to the erudition of the lover and, secondarily, for the sonority of the word Pallas.' And therefore, provided the appropriate sonority is created, the bust could become the bust of one of the nine Muses.

Let us now ask ourselves what would happen if someone wanted to transpose 'The Raven' from a natural language to an image, 'translating' it into a picture. An artist could make us feel emotions similar to those aroused by the poem, such as the darkness of the night, the melancholy atmosphere, the mixture of horror and insatiable desire that churns within the lover, the contrast between black and white (and, if this served to emphasize the effect, the painter could change the bust into a full-figure statue). However, the picture would have to forgo rendering that obsessive feeling of the (reiterated) threat of loss, which is suggested by *nevermore*. Could the picture tell us something of the Lenore who is so frequently invoked in the text? Perhaps, by making her appear to us as a white ghost. But it would have to be the ghost of a woman, not of another creature. And at that point we would be obliged to see (or the painter would be obliged to make us see) something of this woman who in the written text appears as pure sound. In this case, at least, Lessing's distinction between the arts of time and the arts of space holds. And it would hold because in the passage between poetry and picture there has been a *change of continuum*.

I should like to return to Fabbri's observation, which, at first, I had considered an appropriate correction of the identification of interpretation and translation as coextensive concepts. Fabbri pointed out (1998: 117) that 'the true limit of translation would seem to lie in the diversity of the purport of the expression.' The example he gives is a sequence from Fellini's *Orchestra Rehearsal*:

At a certain point there is a character, the orchestra conductor, who is seen from behind. Very soon, however, the spectator notices that the shot introducing this character is a subjective one; the point of view, in fact, is on a level with the line of sight of a person following the conductor's movements, a person who seems to be walking in the conductor's place. Thus far, there is no problem: the point of view is clear; we can translate it into absolutely perfect linguistic terms. But, shortly afterward, the camera overtakes in the shot the character who until that moment was walking ahead of it, until it reaches a point where it is in front of the character. In other words, the camera has overtaken the character whom we first saw from behind and it has slowly but steadily come to a point where he is being filmed from in front. But, do not forget, the shot was a subjective one, a subjectivity that, thanks to the slow and continuous movement of the camera, ends up becoming – without any cut – objective. The character seen from in front is filmed, so to speak, objectively, from the point of view of no one in particular. So the problem is: what happened while the camera was doing this? While the camera was moving round, who was effectively looking? And which category of verbal language is able to render, in other words *to translate*, that intermediate moment (which, although intermediate, is nevertheless slow, continuous, and lasts a certain time) in which the shot has not yet become impersonal but is already no longer subjective?

Although language allows us to say what the camera *did*, the *effect* produced by its movement cannot be fully translated into words.

The diversity of continuum is a fundamental problem for every theory of semiotics. Just think of the diatribe on the *omnipotence* or the *omnieffability* of verbal language. And while we tend to accept verbal language as the most powerful system of all (according to Lotman, it is the *primary modelling system*), we are nonetheless aware that it is not wholly omnipotent. The language of music certainly has limited power compared to speech because it would be rather difficult to express the content of the *Critique of Pure Reason* in music, but a visual language would also have trouble expressing all the senses of Kant's text. Equally, it is difficult to express the sense of Beethoven's *Fifth* in words.[13] The practice of ekphrasis makes it possible to describe an image in words, but no ekphrasis of Raphael's *Wedding of the Virgin* could convey the sense of perspective perceived by the viewer, the flowing lines that manifest the position of the bodies, or the tenuous harmony of the colours.

Moreover, in the passage from purport to purport we are forced to take certain aspects that a translation would leave indeterminate and make them explicit. Take, for example, the images that accompany the German text of Hoffmann's *Struwwelpeter* (a masterpiece of children's illustrations from the nineteenth century), in which it is said that 'Die Sonne lud den Mond zum Essen.' An interlinguistic translation (into Italian) would say that 'il sole invitò la luna a cena' and (into English) that 'the Sun invited the Moon to dinner.' In a translation from German into Italian, we could get round the problem that *Die Sonne* in German is feminine in gender and *Il sole* in Italian is masculine (while *the Sun* in English would not make it necessary to identify the gender). But the text is accompanied by an illustration, which survives as such in every edition in other languages, where the Sun is represented as a lady, and the Moon as a gentleman, and this would seem very strange to Italian readers accustomed to considering the Sun as male and the Moon as a female.

I suggest submitting Dürer's renowned *Die Melancholie* to an English-speaker and to ask if the female figure in the scene is Melancholy itself, or a melancholy woman who symbolizes melancholy. I think our English-speaker would say it was a (melancholy) female figure standing metonymically for that abstract (and asexual) entity that is Melancholy. An Italian and a German would say it was a representation of Melancholy as such, since the Italian *melanconia* (or *malinconia*) and the German *Melancholie* are feminine in gender. Many Italian spectators recall having seen Ingmar Bergmann's *The Seventh Seal*, where Death plays chess with the protagonist. If this had been a written text, *Der Todt* (or its Swedish equivalent, *en dod*, also masculine in gender) would have translated as *La Morte* in Italian (or *La Mort* in French).[14] As Bergmann had to show this Death by means of images, he decided to show it as a male, a fact that strikes every Italian or French spectator, accustomed to conceiving of Death as a being of the female gender. The fact that for Italians and the French this strange and unexpected figure of Death reinforces the impression of fear that the filmic text certainly intended to suggest is, I should say, an 'added value.' But this demonstrates that the transmutation of matter *adds* meaning or lends importance to connotations that were not originally such.

The objection may be raised that every text arouses inferences in its Model Reader, and there is no harm in this if, in the passage from purport to purport, these inferences are made explicit. But we must needs object that (i) if the original text proposed something as an implicit inference, in making that something explicit the text has certainly been *interpreted*, but by leading it to do something overtly that it originally meant to keep implicit; and that (ii) in the case of *The Seventh Seal* the inference ('then this Death is masculine in gender') was not part of the original revelations contained in the text. On the contrary, the text, by depicting Death in male form, did not want to upset the customary connotations determined by the linguistic automatisms of the intended viewer (it did not want to astonish him or her), while the Italian and French versions do exactly the opposite, adding an element of defamiliarization.

The form of the linguistic expression cannot be mapped one to one onto another continuum. In the passage from a verbal language to, let us say, a visual language, there is a comparison between two forms of the expression whose 'equivalences' are not therefore determinable in the same sense that the Italian *settenario doppio*, a double seven-syllable line, is metrically equivalent to the French Alexandrine.

Steiner (1975: 14) reflects on Dante Gabriel Rossetti's translation into poetry of a picture by Ingres, and he concludes that the variations in "meaning" that follow from this ensure that the original picture is seen only as a pretext (we would be in the presence of a case of *rewriting*).[15] What would happen if, in some hypothetical and decidedly fantastic international competition, 'Les chats' were 'translated' into oil paintings by Giotto, Titian, Picasso, and Andy Warhol (and I would add Lorenzo Lotto, who painted an *Annunciation* with a most beautiful cat crossing the room)? And what if it were 'translated' into a tapestry, a cartoon, a bas-relief, or a sculpture in marzipan?

In passing into a semiotic system that is totally 'other' with regard to those of the natural languages, the interpreter would have to decide if the 'savants austères' sit in a large and chilly library, in a cramped little room like one of Rembrandt's philosophers, or in front of a lectern like Saint Jerome, and whether the cat should sit at his feet like the lion before the Father Translator of Holy Writ, and he would have to decide whether the austere sages should wear flowing robes like Holbein's Erasmus, or tight frock coats, and whether austerity should be manifested by flowing white beards or by pince-nez spectacles.

INTERPRETATION, TRANSLATION, AND TRANSMUTATION

I should like to propose an attempt at a different classification of the forms of interpretation, in which due importance is attached to the problems posed by variations in both the substance and the purport of the expression:

1. Interpretation by transcription

2. Intrasystemic interpretation
    2.1. Intralinguistic, within the same natural language
    2.2. Intrasemiotic, within other semiotic systems
    2.3. Performance

3. Intersystemic interpretation
    3.1. With marked variation in the substance
        3.1.1. Interlinguistic, or translation between natural languages
        3.1.2. Rewriting
        3.1.3. Translation between other semiotic systems

    3.2. With mutation of continuum
        3.2.1. Parasynonymy
        3.2.2. Adaptation or transmutation

1. *Interpretation by Transcription*
As we have already said, this is interpretation by automatic substi-
tution, as happens with the Morse alphabet. Transcription is strictly
codified, and may therefore be carried out by a machine. The
absence of interpretative decision and of all reference to the context
or the circumstance of enunciation[16] makes this case of little inter-
est as far as the present discussion is concerned, unless (human)
translators are seen as being on a par with a Turing machine.

2. *Intrasystemic Interpretation*
The interpretants belong to the same semiotic system as the interpreted expression (the same form of the expression). There are, as in

all the cases that follow, variations in the substance of the expression, but they are not very important.

2.1. *Intrasystemic Interpretation within the Same Natural Language*

We have already seen that this category includes all the cases of interpretation of a natural language by means of itself: synonymy, definition, paraphrase, inference, comment, etc., and even parody – insofar as parody is also an admittedly extreme but, in certain cases, highly perspicuous form of interpretation, and it suffices to think of Proust's parodies in *Pastiches et mélanges*, which help to identify the stylistic automatisms, the mannerisms, and the tics of a certain author. In all these cases, the fact that the same content is expressed with different substances is fully admitted for the sake of interpretation – in order always to know something more about the interpretant, as Peirce would have said. To speak of translation in such a case is merely to use a metaphor.

To understand this point better, see in Lepschy 1981 (456–7) the sentence 'His friend could not see the window.' Lepschy observes that this sentence allows for twenty-four different Italian translations, which may combine in a different way a series of choices, namely (i) whether the friend is male or female, (ii) whether *could not* should be understood as an imperfect or a past definite tense, (iii) whether window should be understood as the window of a room (*finestra*) or of a train (*finestrino*) or of a counter, as in a bank teller's window (*sportello*). Lepschy is the first to admit that the twenty-four solutions are only potential, because within the context only one would be appropriate. But this leaves us with three problems, which are very different from one another:

(i)   The twenty-four possibilities exist only as a potential of the linguistic system (and in this sense a good dictionary ought to contain all the possible senses – in other words, all the possible interpretants – of window).

(ii) Confronted with a text that contains this sentence, a reader would have to decide, according to the context, to which story it refers. For example: (a) there is an X who is male; there is a Y who is female; Y is a friend of X; at a precise point in the past, she could not see the window (which X was pointing out to her from the street); (b) there is an X who is male; there is a Y who is male; Y is a friend of X; every time Y went into a bank, he could not identify the teller's window (from which he had to pick up a new cheque book); (c) There is an X who is male; there is a Y who is female; Y is a friend of X; at a precise point in the past, Y could not see the window (of the train); etc. It is clear that this interpretation according to the context is indispensable and is independent of any decision to translate the sentence into another language.

(iii) In order to translate the sentence, let us say, from English into French, the translator must first perform operation (ii). The translation must have this form of *rewording* as a preliminary step, and it must have it precisely because *rewording* is not yet a translation, but in general an intrasystemic interpretation.[17] Only at this point can the translator decide to translate: (a1) 'Son amie ne réussit pas à voir la fenêtre'; (b2) 'Son ami ne réussissait pas à voir le guichet'; (c1) 'Son amie ne réussit pas à voir la fenêtre (du train)'.

2.2. *Intrasystemic Interpretation within Other Semiotic Systems*

We have a second category of intrasystemic interpretations (in systems different from natural languages) when, for example, a musical piece is transcribed in a different key, changing from major to minor or (in ancient times) from the Doric mode to the Phrygian mode, or when a drawing is made with a pantograph, or when a map is reduced in scale or simplified (or, contrariwise, reproduced in greater detail). In these cases, too, the fact that the same content is expressed with different signs leads us to think that the aim is to improve the delimitation of the form of the content (for example, by simplifying a map, making the contours of a country or region more evident), but we are still within the same form of the expression and the same purport of the expression (sonic, visual, etc.). Every time we make a projection on a reduced scale, the substance of the expression changes, as when we define a word, but the change is accepted as not pertinent for the purposes of interpretation.

I would add that in certain cases, for the sake of interpretation, we would be prepared to accept a change of purport, provided it was irrelevant for the purposes of interpretation. Let us suppose that in a school of architecture there is an exhibit featuring a scale model of the Colosseum as it appears today. I have chosen the Colosseum because the model can just as easily show the exterior as the interior, and is therefore didactically perfect. Provided the proportions between the various elements of the model remain unchanged, the reduction in scale is not pertinent. But, as long as the colouring of the surfaces is a reproduction of the real monument, we may maintain that the decision to construct the model in wood, clay, or bronze (and even, if we avail ourselves of the services of highly skilled craftsmen, in marzipan) is not pertinent. In the stores in the centre of Florence, they sell scale-model reproductions of Michelangelo's *David*. If employed for aesthetic enjoyment, such reproductions are obviously disappointing, because the real dimensions are a part of the work of art. But for purposes of recall or study, if the proportional relationships are well reproduced, the matter would become irrelevant, and we would have an acceptable case of intrasystemic interpretation (no worse than someone's telling me that cats are animals that say *miaow*).

2.3. *Performance*

The performance of a musical score or the staging of a ballet or a theatrical piece represent some of the commonest cases of interpretation, to such a point that it is normal practice to talk of musical interpretation, and a good musician is referred to as a good 'interpreter.' For performance as interpretation, I refer the reader to Pareyson 1954. One ought to say that in a performance the same form of the expression is rendered through a change in expressive purport, because what usually happens is that we pass from the notation of a written score (and a theatrical piece can also be called a score) to its realization in sounds, gestures, or words pronounced out loud. But a score is always a set of instructions for the realization of *allographic* works of art, as Goodman (1968) calls them, and therefore it already provides for and prescribes the matter in which the work must be realized, in the sense that the musical page does not only prescribe melody, rhythm, and harmony but also the timbre, and a theatrical text prescribes that the written words must be rendered as vocal sounds (in the case of a passage from a theatrical piece to a ballet, we would instead be dealing with adaptation or transmutation). I have said in Eco 1997 (3.7.8) that a score (like a sonata or a novel) is the token of a type or an infinitely reproducible or 'clonable' *formal individual*. Authors do not rule out that a score can be read without realizing it in sounds, images, or gestures, but in that case too the score suggests how those expressions can be called up mentally. This page is also a score that indicates how it could be read out loud. We can talk about intrasemiotic interpretation because every form of writing is ancillary to the semiotic system it refers to.

Nevertheless, execution is a link between intrasystemic interpretations and intersystemic interpretations with marked variations in the substance, in the sense that between two executions of a sonata for violin or two interpretations of a soliloquy from *Hamlet*, there are pertinent variations of substance with regard to aesthetic judgment (the particular timbre of a Stradivarius, the variations in dynamics, or the timbre of the actor's voice and its particular intonations and the rhythmic scansion of the text). Two directors, with relevant and appreciable variations of substance, can interpret and stage the same classical tragedy using different sets, different costumes, and a different acting style. This also happens, for example, when Mozart's *Don Giovanni* is staged in modern dress, as Peter Brook recently did.

Even though performance is mainly a feature of the *allographic* arts, it may also be found in the autographic arts. New lighting for a picture in an exhibition or a museum can change the way visitors interpret it, and this occurs on the basis of the curator's interpretation. I am tempted to say that cinema directors also 'perform' screenplays, in the sense that the script may say that a character smiles, but the director can make that smile sarcastic or tender, both by instructing the actor and by lighting his or her figure from one angle rather than another. However, I believe that, even though there are some extremely precise screenplays that intend to be highly prescriptive scripts, there are others that would seem to be more like literary rough drafts and in such cases I would speak of adaptation or transmutation.

If, instead, a particular performance is used for purely informative purposes (to identify such and such a sonata, or to know what Hamlet says in his soliloquy), the variations in the substance cease to be pertinent, in the sense that one performance is as good as another.

3. *Intersystemic Interpretation*

3.1. *Intersystemic Interpretations with Marked Variations in the Substance*

There are cases in which interpretation implies important variations in the substance of the expression, and the most obvious case is precisely that of translation proper.

3.1.1. *Translation Proper*

We have already had a good deal to say about this, and we have seen how translation proper ranges from a minimum of attention to the substance to a maximum of its pertinentization, as happens in texts with a poetic function.

3.1.2. *Rewriting*

I would tend to exclude rewriting from the ranks of translations because there is no doubt that it is an anomalous case of translation proper, which falls into the category of intrasystemic interpretations, only insofar as poetic rewriting is admitted within the same language. In such cases, rewriting may even be stretched to include parody. However, since many extremely beautiful poetic pseudo-translations come under this heading, and even though they are attempts at 'transporting' from one natural language to another, I will consider rewriting here, albeit with some qualms. I shall take my example from personal experience, in this case, the problems I faced in my translation of Raymond Queneau's *Exercices de style*. The exercises in question are a series of variations on a basic text.[18] Some are clearly concerned with content (the basic text is modified by litotes, in the form of a prediction, a dream, a press release, etc.) and lend themselves to translation proper. Others, instead, regard expression. In these cases, the basic text is interpreted through *metagraphs* (like anagrams, permutations by an increasing number of letters, lipograms, etc.) or through *metaplasms* (onomatopoeia, syncope, metathesis, etc.). There was nothing else to be done but to rewrite it. If, for example, the challenge the author set himself were to rephrase the basic text without ever using the letter *e*, in an Italian version the same exercise can be performed only if the literal sense of Queneau's variation is not respected. So if the original said, 'Au stop, l'autobus stoppa. Y monta un zazou au cou trop long' ... etc., the Italian would obtain the same effect by saying, 'Un giorno, diciamo alle dodici in punto, sulla piattaforma di coda di un autobus S, vidi un giovanotto dal collo troppo lungo ...'[19]

Queneau's exercises also include references to poetic forms, and in this case too the translation has opted for the most brazen rewriting. Where the original text told the story in Alexandrines, in parodistic reference to the French literary tradition, I took the liberty of telling the same story with an equally parodistic reference to one of Leopardi's cantos. In one variation that in French was based on Italianisms, the translation could only counter-attack by playing on Gallicisms. Finally, the exercise called 'Maladroit' drove me to extremes of free emulation, and the inept speech of an almost aphasic Frenchman became the rambling discourse of a 'freak' during a students' meeting in 1977.

Rewriting occurs in music, with, for example, some types of virtuoso performance (e.g., Liszt's paraphrases of Beethoven's symphonies), or even when the same piece is reworked in a new version by the same composer.

A most particular case of rewriting, taken to extremes, is the Italian translation of that chapter of *Finnegans Wake* entitled 'Anna Livia Plurabelle.' Although this translation appeared originally under the names of Frank and Settanni, who certainly contributed to the work, it should be considered as the work of Joyce himself.[20] Similarly, the French translation of 'Anna Livia,' which was made in collaboration with many writers like Beckett, Soupault, and others, is also now considered to be mostly Joyce's work.[21] I shall refer to these translations from now on as ItJoyce and FrJoyce.

Finnegans Wake is not written in English, but in 'Finneganian,' which some have defined as an invented language. In reality, it is not an invented language like Chlebnikov's transmental language, or the poetic languages of Morgenstern and Hugo Ball, where no translation is possible, because the phonosymbolic effect depends precisely on the absence of any semantic level – and therefore it is pointless to translate. *Finnegans Wake* is more of a plurilingual text. Consequently, it would be just as pointless to translate it, because it is already translated. Translating it, given a pun containing the English radical T and an Italian radical I, would at best be like translating the syntagm TI into the syntagm IT. And this is what many translators have tried to do, with varying results.

The fact remains that *Finnegans Wake* is not even a plurilingual text: or, rather, it is, but from the standpoint of the English language. It is a plurilingual text written as an English-speaker conceived of one. It seems to me therefore that Joyce's decision to translate himself was based on the idea of thinking of the target text (French or Italian) as a plurilingual text the way a French- or Italian-speaker might have conceived of one.

Thus, if – as Humboldt had already suggested – translating means not only leading the reader to understand the language and culture of the original but also enriching one's own, there can be no doubt that in every translation of *Finnegans Wake*, insofar as it leads the language to express what it was unable to express before (just as Joyce had done with English), translation makes the language take a step forward. It may be that the step is an excessive one, that the language cannot stand the experiment, but something has happened in the meantime.

ItJoyce found himself having to render a language that lends itself to pun, to neologisms, and agglutination, as well as English does (which has the advantage of an abundance of monosyllabic terms) into a language like Italian, which resists the formation of agglutinative neologisms. Faced with German expressions like *Kunstwissenschaft* or *Frauprofessor*, Italian surrenders. Just as it does when confronted with *splash-down*. It takes refuge in the highly poetic *ammarare* (which indicates the gentle landing of a hydrofoil, but not the forceful impact of a space capsule with the surface of the sea). On the other hand, every language has its own distinctive character: for moon landings, English makes improper use of the verb *to land*, while Italian has invented *allunare*. Fine. But if we were translating a text in which there is an exciting passage describing a spaceship landing, *land* would be a monosyllable, while *alluna* is a trisyllable. This would pose problems of rhythm.

Let us take a look right away at an example in which Joyce, forced to translate a rhythm proper to English, reformulates a text to adapt it first to the French language and then to Italian:

> Tell me all, tell me now. You'll die when you hear. Well, you know, when the old cheb went futt and did what you know. Yes, I know, go on.

Here there are thirty monosyllabic words. The French version tries to reproduce the same monosyllabic structure, at least from an oral standpoint:

> Dis-moi tout, dis-moi vite. C'est à en crever. Alors, tu sais, quand le vieux gaillard fit krack et fit ce que tu sais. Oui je sais, et après, après?

Twenty-five monosyllables. Not bad. The remainder consists of words made up of only two and, at most, three syllables. What happens with Italian, a language with few monosyllabic words, compared to English at any rate?

Dimmi tutto, e presto presto. Roba da chiodi! Beh, sai quando il messercalzone andò in rovuma e fe' ciò che fe'? Sì, lo so, e po' appresso?

Sixteen monosyllables, but at least half of them are conjunctions, articles, and prepositions, 'proclitic particles,' which have no tonic accent, but are bound to the following word and, if anything, from the point of view of the auditory effect, lengthen it. All the other words are of two, three, or even four or five syllables. The rhythm of the passage is not monosyllabic at all. Where the English text arguably has a jazzy rhythm, the Italian has an operatic flavour. This was Joyce's decision. If we take a look at other passages from his Italian version, we find some extremely long words like *scassavillani*, *lucciolanterna* and *pappapanforte, freddolesimpellettate, inapprodabile*, and *vezzeggiativini* – long even for the Italian lexicon, and, in fact, Joyce invented them.

Of course, *Finnegans Wake* also uses some very long compound words, but the play is usually on the fusion of two short words. Since Italian does not lend itself to this solution, Joyce opted for the opposite choice: he sought a polysyllabic rhythm. In order to obtain this result, he was seldom bothered if the Italian text said different things from the English text.

Let us give a very significant example. Toward the end of the second passage translated, both by FrJoyce and ItJoyce, we find:

Latin me that, my trinity scholard, out of eure sanscreed into oure eryan!

Without wishing to seek out all the allusions, I find that some strike us immediately. There are two linguistic references, to Latin and Sanskrit, whose Aryan origins are stressed. There is the Holy Trinity but also *sans*-creed (and we should remember that the Arian heresy hinged on the doctrine of the Trinity), and one notices Erin in the background, and Trinity College. In addition, but only for manic philologists, there is a reference to the rivers Ure, Oure, and Eure (and we shall be considering the role of rivers in *Finnegans Wake* later). FrJoyce decided to keep faith with the central associative nucleus (although much was lost) and translates:

Latine-moi ça mon prieux escholier, de vostres sanscroi en notre erryen.

Granted that the chain of association *prieur-pieux-prière* holds an echo of the Trinity, in *sanscroi* the reference is both to Sanskrit and to *sans croix* and *sans foi*, and in *erryen* there is a certain allusion to error or to errancy.

And now let us move on to ItJoyce. Here the author has evidently decided that the linguistic references had to pass, so to speak, from linguistics to the glossa or from language to tongue, understood as a physical organ; and that any theological errancy had to become sexual errancy:

Latinami ciò, laureata di Cuneo, da lingua aveta in gargarigliano.

Any translator who was not Joyce himself would have been accused of intolerable licence. Of course there is licence, and it is almost sophomoric in tone, but it is sanctioned by the author. The only reference to archaic languages is in that *aveta-avita*, which however, in the light of what follows, also evokes an *avis avuta*. As for the rest, the female graduate from Cuneo (which is a toponym, but also means 'wedge') has been penetrated by a wedge of sorts, because if the syntagm *Cuneo-da-lingua* is pronounced rapidly there emerges an echo of *cunnilingus*, reinforced by the allusion to gargling that ends, however, without the authorization of the original, with a reference to the 801st river of the 800 rivers mentioned in this chapter, the Garigliano.

The Trinity has vanished and Joyce calmly consummates his ultimate apostasy. What he wanted to do was to show what could be done with Italian, not with the *Filioque*. The theme was a pretext.

Some of the lessons we learn from both FrJoyce and ItJoyce apply to any translation, whether it be source- or target-oriented. One of the characteristics that make this passage a celebrated one in the world of Joyce scholarship is that, in order to convey the feeling of the flow of the river Liffey, it contains the names – variously disguised – of roughly 800 rivers.[22] It is a real *tour-de-force*, which often does not introduce any phonosymbolic enhancement to the piece, but rests entirely on the semantic, or encyclopedic, side. Those who grasp the references to the various rivers are better equipped to grasp the feeling of the Liffey flowing by. But since not everyone can grasp the references to the rivers Chebb, Futt, Bann, Duck, Sabrainn, Till, Waag, Bomu, Boyana, Chu, Batha, Skollis, Shari and so on, it is all, so to speak, up to the almost statistical play of associations: if you catch the name of some rivers you know, you sense fluidity; if you do not, not to worry, it remains a private wager on the author's part, and a subject for a doctoral thesis. So much so that, in the first version of the rivers, there were very few of them indeed. But there is a spate of them in the subsequent versions, and it seems that at that point Joyce called in outside help to help find as many of them as possible. All they had to do was get down to work with encyclopedias and atlases, and then the business of making a pun was not that difficult. Let us say therefore that whether the chapter contains 800 or 200 rivers is irrelevant – or, at least, it is as irrelevant as the fact that Renaissance painters painted, among the faces in a crowd, the faces of their friends: so much the better for the academic career of those who manage to identify them all, but in order to enjoy the painting or the fresco, it counts only up to a certain point.

ItJoyce takes a triple decision. The first is source-oriented. It is necessary to make it clear that the chapter is lexically, and not merely syntactically, fluvial, and is based on numerous references to rivers. But these do not necessarily have to be in the same places in which they appear in the original. For example, in the English text, after Wasserbourne (which in ItJoyce is cancelled by a *Wassermanschift*), there appears a *Havemmarea* (*Ave Maria* + *marea*, or tide), which would have been very easy to render in Italian, all the more so because the Havel is a German river that flows into the Elbe. But Joyce has already played with the hint of the Ave Maria fifteen or so lines before, introducing (where it does not appear in the English text) a *Piavemarea* (the river Piave plus *marea*)! By way of compensation, one sentence later, we read that there is *poca schelda* (scelta = choice + *Schelda*, or Scheldt), and here the Scheldt is recovered from an English page that is not a part of the passages translated.

Where the English text has the Rio Negro and La Plata, ItJoyce retains them, but introduces a *mosa*. And so on, according to the taste and inspiration of the author translating himself.

Second decision, this time target-oriented and domesticating. With names like Sui, Tom, Chef, Syr Darya, or Ladder Burn, it is possible to indulge in some fine wordplay in English, but it is harder to do this in Italian. ItJoyce drops what he cannot use and instead introduces some Italian rivers, more obvious for his new reader, and more suited to the composition of refined polysyllables. Hence we find (in the Italian, but not in the English) the rivers Serio, Po, Serchia, Piave, Conca, Aniene, Ombrone, Lambro, Taro, Toce, Belbo, Sillaro, Tagliamento, Lamone, Brembo, Trebbio, Mincio, Tidone, Panaro (indirectly the Tanaro), and perhaps the Orba (as *orva*), and the willing reader is free to go off in search of them beneath their various guises.[23]

But there are not enough rivers in Italy, and since the names of many countries in the world did not lend themselves to compositions resembling Italian, Joyce, with supreme nonchalance, deleted a great number of rivers that appear in the original. In the portion of English text translated both by FrJoyce and ItJoyce there are 277 rivers, including a fine allusion to the two banks of the Seine (*Reeve Gootch* and *Reeve Drughad*, and one to the Kattegat). ItJoyce's solution is to go from 277 to 74 rivers (allowing the translator a generic *rio*, a *fiumana*, and a *comaschia* that combines Lake Como and the swamps of Comacchio, albeit still connected with the delta of a river, and finally the *maremme Tolkane*).

There is no reason for the elimination of so many rivers. It is not for reasons of comprehensibility. Especially because names like Honddu, Zwaerte, or Kowsha ought to be as incomprehensible to English readers as they are to their Italian counterparts, and if an English reader can put up with 277, why not the Italian reader? And also because while ItJoyce keeps some rivers that appear in English, he does not seem to respect any criterion of perspicuity. Why does ItJoyce translate 'and the dneepers of wet and the gangres of sin' as 'com'è gangerenoso di turpida tabe'? It was a fine piece of work to introduce the Rhine (*Reno*) into the Ganges, but why drop the Dnieper? Why avoid the Merrimack (in 'Concord on the Merrimake') to render it as 'O in nuova Concordia dell'Arciponente,' where we arguably gain a celestial allusion to the Almighty (*Onnipotente*), but by keeping a Concord that is no longer recognizable as the one on the Merrimack, while losing, for what it was worth, the reference to the places of American transcendentalism? Only to keep, with 'Sabrinettuccia la fringuellina,' an allusion to the Sabrainn, which is a mere bauble with which to adorn a Ph.D. thesis? Why preserve the (extremely recondite) references to the Boyarka, the Bua, the Boyana, and the Büech, which run God only knows where, and drop the Sambre, the Euphrates, the Oder, and the Neisse?[24]

It is clear that Joyce, in collaborating with ItJoyce, sang to himself, so to speak, melodramatically sonorous possible Italian neologisms, discarding those that did not sound right to his mental ear, and that he was practically no longer interested in rivers. No longer playing with the idea of rivers (perhaps the oddest and most punctilious idea in this punctilious and extravagant book), he was playing with Italian instead. He had spent almost ten years looking for 800 rivers, and he discarded nearly nine-tenths of them to be able to say *chiacchiericcianti, baleneone, quinciequindi,* and *frusciacque.*

ItJoyce is certainly not an example of 'faithful' translation. Yet many have written that, to understand *Finnegans Wake,* it would be a good idea to start with his Italian translation of it. Perhaps, or rather certainly because, on seeing the text wholly rethought in another language, one can understand its deep mechanisms, over and beyond the insistence on this or that play of quotations.

Here is one final example of rewriting that stands at the limits of the original creation:

> Tell us in franca langua. And call a spate a spate. Did they never sharee you ebro at skol, you antiabecedarian? It's just the same as if I was to go par examplum now in conservancy's cause out of telekinesis and proxenete you. For coxyt sake and is that what she is?

Call a spate a spate is nicely ironic insofar as it suggests the colloquial invitation to talk plainly without any frills, while there is also another fluvial connotation, in this case a flood of speech. *Sharee* unites *share* and the river Shari, *ebro* unites *Hebrew* and the Ebro, skol unites *school* and the river Skollis. To skip other references, *for coxyt sake* brings to mind the infernal river Cocytus as well as *for God's sake* (and therefore an invocation, in this context, that is blasphemous).[25] FrJoyce solves the last invocation with an allusion to blasphemy, as *nom de flieuve.* ItJoyce translates:

Dillo in lingua franca. E chiama piena piena. T'hanno mai imparato l'ebro all'iscuola, antebecedariana che sei? E' proprio siccome circassi io a mal d'esempio da tamigiaturgia di prossenetarti a te. Ostrigotta, ora capesco.

Faced with the difficulty of rendering the allusions of the original, here the translator-author decides to recuperate (via thaumaturgy) those two rivers mentioned elsewhere, the Thames (*Tamigi* in Italian) and, with that *piena piena*, Pian Creek, Piana, and Pienaars that appear in the original two pages later. But it should also be remembered that *to call a spate a spate* translates into Italian as 'dire pane al pane' (to call bread bread), and here *pane* is suggested by the word *piena* (flood). But this is not enough for Joyce the author-translator. He is aware that the deep meaning of the passage, over and beyond the play of quotation and reference, is that of a perplexed and diabolic uncertainty in the face of the mysteries of a *lingua franca* that, like all its ilk, derives from different languages and does not answer to the distinctive character of any of them, leaving the impression of a diabolic plot against the one and only true and unattainable language, which would be, if it existed, the *lingua sancta*. With the result that every antiabecedarian heresiarch is antitrinitarian and anti-other-things-too (Circassian, and barbarian, into the bargain). And so he decides to get out from under with a piece of brilliant self-translation: 'Ostrigotta, ora capesco' (which does not appear in the original text).

We have an exclamation of disappointment and amazement, *ostregheta* (literally little oyster, but also a euphemism for the blasphemous oath in the dialect of the Veneto 'ostia!' literally 'by the host!'), a suggestion of incomprehensible languages, *ostrogoto* (Ostrogothic: a sylloge of the whole of *Finnegans Wake*), and *Gott* (God). Blasphemy pronounced before an incomprehensible tongue. And so it would seem right to end with *non capisco* (I do not understand). But *ostrigotta* also suggests *I got it*, and as ItJoyce writes *ora capesco*, which is a blend of *capisco* (I understand) and *esco* (I get out), Joyce gets out from under the problem, or the *meandertale*.

The truth is that Joyce did not care a whit for any of our translation problems. What he wanted to do was invent an expression like 'Ostrigotta, ora capesco.'

In conclusion, rewriting is certainly a case of interpretation, and is translation proper only in part, if not in the sense in which (on the basis of a critical interpretation of the original text) it has pretensions to conveying, not the letter of the original, but its 'guiding spirit' (whatever that means).

3.1.3. *Intersystemic Interpretation with Very Marked Differences in Substance among Non-linguistic Systems*

Think, for example, of the printed reproduction of a pictorial work, where the continuous texture of the painted surface is translated in terms of a typographical screen. In the nineteenth century, in the absence of more refined typographical processes, a skilful engraver would 'translate' *al tratto* an oil painting, a fresco, or an illuminated manuscript into black and white. These are cases in which the interpretant says less than the expression interpreted (there is, for example, the loss of the colour), but it might also be decided that in some way *it said more* because it adapted the original image to the tastes of its own addressees, with the result that a medieval illuminated manuscript and a Renaissance painting had a nineteenth-century appearance.

It is a matter for debate in such cases as to whether there is not also a change of continuum, but it is assumed that source text and target text manifest themselves within a common continuum that we will call graphic-pictorial. However, I would have no difficulty in taking the 'translation' of an oil picture into a monochromatic engraving as a case of change in continuum, and therefore of adaptation or transmutation.

Instead, many of Viollet-le-Duc's neogothic reconstructions – which were intended to be faithful revivals of non-extant medieval sculpture or stained-glass work – should be seen as intrasystemic translations dominated by an attempt at *modernization*, insofar as, although the *material* (stone) remains the same and the author's intention is to be faithful, they are romantic interpretations of medieval taste.

A particular case of a variation in the substance while remaining within the same semiotic system (and therefore on the boundary between intrasystemic and intersystemic interpretations, but at a point where one may consider it a translation) is what happens, for example, with the transcription for recorder of Bach's *Suites for Solo Cello*. This is an excellent interpretation that preserves, in the decided change of timbre, most of the musical values of the original piece – for example, by 'translating' into an arpeggio the chords made on the cello by drawing the bow across several strings simultaneously.

3.2. *Intersystemic Interpretation with Mutation of Continuum*
In these cases there is a decided step from purport to the purport of the expression, as happens when a poem is interpreted (by illustrating it) through a charcoal drawing, or when a novel is adapted in comic-strip form.

3.2.1. *Parasynonymy*
I cannot find a better term for cases like the one, already mentioned, in which an object is shown in order to interpret a verbal expression that nominates it, a pointing finger that makes clear the expression *that one there*, a verbal instruction that expresses the meaning of a one-way street sign.[26] In this case, the object held up

is certainly intended to interpret the linguistic expression, but in different circumstances of utterance the same object could also interpret different expressions. One example of parasynonymy would be the showing of an empty box of a given detergent to interpret (to make clearer) the request 'Please buy me a box of Brand X detergent,' but in different circumstances of utterance holding up the same thing could clarify the meaning of the word *detergent* (in general) or provide an example of what is meant by *parallelepipedon*.

3.2.2. *Adaptation or Transmutation*

The commonest cases have to do with the adaptation of a novel to film, or occasionally to theatre, but there are cases of the adaptation of a fairy tale for a ballet or, as in Walt Disney's *Fantasia*, of classical music for animated cartoons. There are frequent instances, albeit inspired by commercial criteria, of adaptations of films to novels. There are many variations, but we ought always to talk of adaptation or transmutation for the reasons that follow, and precisely in order to distinguish these interpretations from translation proper.

3.2.2.1. *In absentia and in praesentia*

A translation proper can be made both in the presence of the original text and in its absence. Translations *in absentia* are more common (and this applies to every foreign novel read in one's own language), but translations with the original text on the facing page are translations *in praesentia*. This decision on the publisher's part does not change the meaning or the value of the translation, and at most the text on the facing page introduces elements useful for appraising its worth. Nobody would think that a translation with the original on the facing page would justify cuts or manipulation or any particular licence just because the reader can always refer to the original text.

It is a different matter with adaptations. For example, the adaptation of a musical piece for ballet involves the simultaneous presence of music (source text) and choreographic action (target text) in such a way that they support each other reciprocally, and the action alone without the support of the music would not seem like an adaptation of anything. Likewise music alone without action would not be a translation but the re-execution of a musical piece. An adaptation for ballet of Chopin's *Funeral March* (from the Sonata in B flat minor, op. 35) evidently has us see things that it would be venturesome to attribute to the musician and that belong to the inferences made by the choreographer.

Nobody would deny that such interpretations also serve to help us appreciate the source work better. We could speak of *understanding through manipulation*.

3.2.2.2. *Understanding through Manipulation*

Let us take a look at some of the operations carried out by Walt Disney in *Fantasia*. Some have always seemed kitsch responses in which renowned compositions are seen as purely descriptive, and descriptive according to the most popular vulgate. Undoubtedly, interpreting Beethoven's *Pastoral* as a story of the vagaries of the weather, on the one hand, and unicorns prancing about on grassy meadows, on the other, is calculated to make Hanslick turn in his grave. Nevertheless, Disney's manipulation is intended as an interpretation of that embarrassing title, *Pastoral*, which the composition must perforce carry like a label, and which undoubtedly induces many listeners to interpret it descriptively. Likewise, adapting *The Rite of Spring* as if it were a history of the earth, and the story of dinosaurs condemned to extinction, is a highly debatable interpretation. However, it cannot be denied that, by *manipulating* the source, Disney suggests a 'barbaric' reading of Stravinsky's composition, and it would be hard to deny that the way Disney chose to adapt the *Rite* is more legitimate than a hypothetical adaptation in which the unicorns of the *Pastoral* were superimposed over the *Rite* (or, vice-versa, if the dinosaurs of the *Rite* were superimposed over the music of Beethoven).

Some have noted that while Disney's adaptation of Tschaikovsky's *Nutcracker Suite* – in which rhythms, timbre, and musical phrases are interpreted in terms of leaves, garlands, elves, and dewdrops – certainly manipulates the source using elements that are not ascribable to the intentions of the original text (no matter how descriptive it was meant to be), it nonetheless fixes the listeners' attention on effective musical values and therefore leads them to appreciate mainly the timbre, the rhythms, and the melodic intentions of the composition (see Cano and Cremonini 1990). As with all interpretations, this adaptation is a matter for debate, but this often holds true also for the gestures of the orchestra conductor who moves his hands and arms emphatically, sometimes sol-faing under his breath, or puffing, or roaring, in order to induce the musicians to grasp the way in which the composition should be executed, *according to his interpretation.* The conductor's gestures are an interpretation of the score. Nobody would dare to say that they are a translation of it in the sense in which the transcription of *Suites for Solo Cello* into suites for alto recorder is.

3.2.2.3. *Showing Things Left Unsaid*

In chapter 10 of *The Betrothed,* after having spoken at length about the contemptible Egidio's seduction of the Nun of Monza, Manzoni, in a passage of great discretion and modesty, makes evident the nun's fall from grace with one very brief sentence: 'La sventurata rispose' (the poor wretch answered).[27]

Later, the novel goes on to deal with the Lady's change of attitude, and her progressive downward slide into criminal conduct. But what happened between the moment of the answer and what ensued thereafter (from the point of view of the linear manifestation of the text) is not mentioned. The author tells us that the nun has succumbed, and the gravity of her succumbing is suggested by that *sventurata* (poor wretch) and its sense of both a severe moral judgment and a feeling of human compassion. It is the cooperation of the reader, called upon to give that reticence a 'voice,' which makes that short sentence the source of a variety of illations. Note that the power of the sentence does not lie only in its icasticity, but also in its rhythm. In this case, we have a double dactyl followed by a spondee (or trochee, because *ultima syllaba non curatur*): -- ∪∪, -- ∪∪, -- --.

A French translation[28] gives 'L'infortunée répondit,' and together with the semantic values it has retained a metrically similar solution ∪ -- ∪∪, -- ∪∪, -- ∪. The English translation, 'The poor wretch answered him,' is more or less -- ∪, -- ∪∪. Along with the semantic values, I think that a certain rhythm has been retained. Anyhow, in both cases, the stylistic value of icasticity has emerged unscathed.

What would happen if that page were to be translated into film – indeed, what did happen, seeing as Manzoni's novel has been the subject of various versions for both television and cinema?[29] All we need do is carry out a mental experiment: no matter how discreet or modest the director may be, he would have *to show us* something more than the written text does. Between Egidio's first conversation with the Lady and her subsequent crimes, that 'answer' must manifest itself through some actions, whether they are suggested by a gesture, a smile, a gleam in the eye, a tremor – if not more. In any case, we *would see* something of the intensity of the answer, which the written text left indeterminate. Out of the nebula of the woman's possible acts of passion, one would be chosen as the most appropriate, while Manzoni evidently wanted it to remain the reader's inalienable right to make a choice, or not to make any, as compassion would suggest.

Let us suppose there is a novel that tells the story of two friends who, during the Terror, are both taken to the guillotine – one because he was a Vendéan legitimist, the other because he was a friend of Robespierre, who had by that time fallen from grace. The novel tells us that both men go to the block with impassible mien but, through some things left unsaid and some carefully calibrated hints, it leaves us uncertain as to whether each of them, on his way to death, is disowning his own past or not. What the novel wants to convey is precisely the climate of uncertainty and moral disorientation in which all were immersed in that terrible '93.

Now let us turn the scene into film. Let us grant that the impassibility of the two condemned men can be rendered, and that their faces do not betray any emotion, either remorse or pride. But whereas the novel does not say how the two were dressed, the film must show them dressed in some way. Will the legitimist wear the culottes and the tunic that were the mark of his caste, thereby underlining the values in which he had believed? Will the Jacobin be defiantly shirtless? Will (improbable, but not impossible) the roles be reversed, with the Jacobin rediscovering his aristocratic pride in culottes while the Vendéan has abandoned all identity? Will both be dressed the same way, thereby emphasizing the fact that both are (and feel themselves to be) equal, victims of the same conflict?

As can be seen, in shifting to another purport, the spectator of the film is obliged to accept an interpretation with regard to which the reader of the novel enjoyed far more freedom. This does not mean that, through its own medium, the film cannot manage to recover the ambiguity before or after that scene, perhaps at a point where the novel was more explicit. But it implies a manipulation that only the foolhardy would designate as translation.

Let us go back to a personal experience. In writing *The Name of the Rose*, which is set in a medieval abbey, I described nocturnal scenes, indoor scenes, and scenes in the open. I did not prescribe a general chromatic tone for the entire story. When the novel was 'translated' into a movie by Jean-Jacques Annaud, he asked my opinion on this point. I told him that the Middle Ages represented itself, especially in illuminated manuscripts, in crude and glaring colours, that it saw itself with little shading, and preferred light and clarity. I cannot recall if in writing I was thinking of those colours, and I admit that readers can colour certain scenes as they will, each reader recreating his or her own medieval ambience in the imagination.

When I eventually saw the film, my first reaction was that my Middle Ages had become 'Caravaggesque,' and therefore seven-teenth-century, with a few gleams of warm light against dark back-grounds. In my heart, I mourned a considerable misinterpretation of the *intentio operis*. It was only later, on reflecting, that I under-stood that the director had conducted himself, I should say, in a natural manner. If the scene unfolds in a closed place, illuminated by a torch or a lantern, or by the light from a single window (and outside it is night, or foggy), the result obtained can only be Caravaggesque, and what little light does strike the faces suggests more Georges de la Tour than *Les très riches heures du duc de Berry* or Ottonian illuminated manuscripts. Perhaps the medieval period portrayed itself in clear and glaring colours, but, in fact, it saw itself for the greater part of the day in Baroque *chiaroscuri*. No objec-tions, except that the film was obliged to make decisions where the novel did not. By making this decision, the director opted for a 'realistic' reading and let other possibilities lapse. In the novel, the lantern was *flatus vocis*, and the intensity of its light was entirely up to the imagination; in the film, the lantern became luminous matter and it expressed precisely that luminous intensity and no other.

In the shift from continuum to continuum, the interpretation is mediated by the adapter, and is not left at the mercy of the addressee.

3.2.2.4. *Isolating a Level of the Text*

Naturally, it may be observed (see Dusi 1999, for example) that many adaptations are translations in the sense that they isolate one of the levels of the source text, and it is this level that the adapter wishes to render in another continuum. The most common example is a film that takes a novel and isolates the narrative level, the sequence of events, and may drop (or merely try to emulate in another continuum) its stylistic aspects. Or the same film may set out to render in another continuum the pathematic effects of the source text, perhaps even at the expense of literal faithfulness to the story. In trying to render the pangs of the narrator in Proust's *Recherche* when, at the beginning, he is waiting for his mother's goodnight kiss, those things that were inner feelings can be rendered with facial expressions (or quasi-dreamlike insertions of the mother figure, who is only desired in the text and not seen). In this sense, an adaptation would be similar to forms of poetic translation where, in order to preserve the rhyme or the metrical scheme, for example, we are prepared to compromise on other aspects. But, when a poet translates another poet, all we are prepared to allow is that, if the translator lays the maximum stress on emulation at the expense of literal faithfulness, then we are dealing with a case of rewriting, which is, within the same purport of the expression, the procedure closest to adaptation or transmutation.

Let us also assume that in an adaptation some levels – deemed fundamental – are isolated, and it is on these levels that we try to 'translate.' But the fact of having isolated some levels means *imposing one's own interpretation of the source text*. Anyone who in 'translating' *The Betrothed* into film wished to render faithfully only the sequence of events, in dropping the ironic-moralistic observations that have such a major part to play in Manzoni's work, would have in fact decided that the sequence of events has priority over the ethical intention and, what is more, that the sequence of events also has priority over the intention to make the ethical purpose emerge through the numerous 'intrusions' of the narrator. A translation proper (from language to language) would have instead to save the two levels at all costs, and leave the reader free to think (let us say) that the moralistic level is predominant – to such a point that one could maintain that the effect of the novel would not change even if don Rodrigo died from a riding accident and not of plague, and even if don Rodrigo, and not the Unnamed, were to convert, while the latter dies unrepentant in the lazar house.

Therefore adaptations always constitute a *critical standpoint*, even if an unconscious one, even if due to lack of skill rather than a deliberate interpretative choice. Naturally, a translation proper also implies, with an interpretation, a critical standpoint. As we have seen, the translators that respected the lapidary brevity of 'the poor wretch replied' implicitly recognized (and emphasized in their own way) the extent to which that lapidary brevity was stylistically important. But in translation the critical attitude of the translator is in fact implicit, and tends be concealed, while in adaptation it becomes preponderant and constitutes the very essence of the process of transmutation.

3.2.2.5. *Adaptation as a New Work*

A typical example of this is *The Orchestra*, a film by Zbig Rybczynski (see the analysis of the film in Basso 1999), where the music of Chopin's funeral march (executed *in praesentia*) is 'shown' at the same time through a series of grotesque figures that appear gradually, as they place their hands on a piano keyboard that runs on for a very long time, as if it were moving along the screen (or as if the camera were tracking along a sequence of keys of infinite length). We are certainly dealing with an attempt to render the source music in some way, because the gestures of the characters are determined by the rhythm of the piece, and the images, including certain things that appear in the background (for example, a hearse), are intended to convey a funereal effect. But the director could have shown an infinity of George Sand clones, or skulls, in a sort of *Totentanz*, while still respecting the rhythmic structure of the piece and giving a visual equivalent of the minor key, and nobody could say, in theory, whether one choice was better than the other. With *The Orchestra*, we find ourselves confronted with an authentic interpretation that, if it were understood as a 'faithful' translation of Chopin's piece, would certainly pose some problems of musicological correctness. This is a work that is good in and of itself, even though the reference to Chopin is an integral part of it.

The film takes its cue not only from Chopin but also, among others, Ravel and his *Bolero*. Here the obsessive nature of the music is rendered by a succession of extremely long uninterrupted sequences of curious characters shot from one side on an endless stairway. There is no doubt that this establishes a certain parallelism between musical reiteration and visual reiteration. But the characters ascending the stairs are taken from Soviet revolutionary iconography (ironically reinterpreted), and this interpretation is entirely the merit (or demerit) of the director, not of Ravel. In the end, the matter for aesthetic appreciation is the (original) work of Rybczynski.

If the director had shown, to the solemn and majestic rhythm of Chopin's funeral march, a French cancan, we would no longer talk even of an adaptation but of a provocative parody.

Confronted with an imaginary book written by Chopin and translated by Rybczynski, we would first of all appreciate Chopin's art, and then Rybczynski's skill, so much so that the publisher would put Chopin's name on the cover and that of Rybczynski (usually) on the frontispiece, and in a smaller type than Chopin's. If the book were awarded a literary prize (which was not a prize for the best translation), it would be assigned to Chopin and not to Rybczynski. If Rybczynski were to appear in a concert hall and execute Chopin's funeral march on the piano, even if the posters showed the performer's name in larger letters than that of the name of the composer whose work was being performed, we would ask Rybczynski to execute Chopin's score according to the dictates of his own inspiration, but without disturbing the performance with theatrical gestures, grimaces, or laughter, while wearing a mask, or showing off a hairy chest or a tattooed back. If he were to do any of these things, we would know we were in the presence of a theatrical action, a performance by means of which – as they used to say – the actor means to make a 'spoof' of a work of art.

But in the case of *The Orchestra*, it is above all the name of Rybczynski, and not that of Chopin or Ravel, which rightly dominates the opening credits. Rybczynski is the author of the film whose subject is the visual adaptation of its own soundtrack, and – except for some cantankerous music lovers – spectators do not trouble to judge whether the execution of the soundtrack is better or worse than other executions of Chopin, but focus their attention on the way in which Rybczynski interprets the musical stimulus through images.

I do not think it can be said that *The Orchestra* is simply a translation of Chopin's composition, as would be the case with transpositions into other keys or even (no matter how debatable) a transcription for organ. It is certainly a work by Rybczynski that has taken its cue from Chopin in order to produce something highly original. The fact that *The Orchestra* might offend the sensibilities of Chopin devotees is entirely secondary.

BORDERLINE CASES

The same devotees would be equally offended by an execution of Chopin's funeral march made by a New Orleans jazz band. Would this also be a case of adaptation or transmutation? No, because there would be no mutation of matter. But the considerable alterations in rhythm and timbre would rule this out as a case of simple transcription, as happens when Bach's *Suites* are modified for recorder rather than cello. Mirka Danuta[30] has drawn my attention to a series of 'musical translations,' many of which I have mentioned, while for others it is legitimate to wonder whether they are not borderline cases, or whether they are, with regard to my table, transversal. Think of the *variation*, which is certainly an interpretation of the theme, and lies within the same semiotic system, but is certainly not a translation because it develops, it amplifies, and – of course – it varies (apart from the fact that there is a difference between a variation on one's own theme and a variation on someone else's theme). Think, too, of the different *harmonizations* obtained from the same piece in the musical tradition of the Protestant Church, where there is not only a variation in substance, but an intense enhancement of the harmonic texture of the composition.

All I have tried to do in my table is to establish some macroscopic distinctions, as I am well aware that there will always be an overlap between one category of the typology and another. Such zones will be imprecise and of a kind liable to generate endless subcategories, at least until such time as we are free to think up infinite forms of interpretation of a text.

But the fact that there can be many nuances in the wealth of semiosis does not mean that it is inadvisable to establish the basic distinctions. On the contrary, it is essential, if the task of semiotic analysis is that of identifying different phenomena in the apparently uncontrollable flux of interpretative acts.

NOTES

1 See, for example, how in *CP* 2.89 *translation* is used, together with *transaction*, *transfusion*, and *transcendental*, as that which can be 'suggested' by the term *Transuasion*, indicating Thirdness as mediation, insofar as different from Originality (or Firstness, 'being such as that being is, regardless of aught else') and from Obstinence (as Secondness).

2 David Savan, certainly one of the most perceptive interpreters of Peirce, remarked that 'according to Peirce, interpretation is a translation' (1988: 17). However, in his analysis of all the forms of interpretation, he does not use the notion of translation any longer. On the contrary, he understands very clearly that not every interpretation is similar to an interlinguistic translation.

3 I use *purport*, in accordance with the English version of Hjelmslev 1943, but Fabbri uses the word *materia*, in the sense of a 'material continuum that is to be segmented by a given Form of Expression,' as we shall see later.

4 In Cortelazzo-Zolli, *Dizionario etimologico* (Bologna: Zanichelli, 1999), we are told that *tradurre* in the sense of 'to transport from one language to another' appears in Varchi 1565.

5 In Roman Jakobson, *Language in Literature*, ed. Krystyna Pomorska and Stephen Rudy (Cambridge: Harvard UP, 1987).

6 *I fiori del male* (Milan: Mursia, 1974).

7 'Fedeli d'amore' suggests the idea of the legendary sect to which Dante is said to have belonged, but evidently Bonfantini hoped, not without reason, that this erudite connotation would not be apparent to the majority of readers.

8 If we look at the rest of the translation, we may notice how in the second quatrain Bonfantini faithfully respects the *abba* variation, albeit by opting for an assonance instead of a rhyme, and he renders the remaining two triplets (*aab, cbc*) with *aab, cdc*, thus introducing a licence that it might have been possible to avoid. But this is a small flaw in an excellent translation.

9 *Poésies complètes* (Paris: Mercure de France, 1910).

10 Fernando Pessoa, 'O corvo,' *Athena* 1, October 1924. See *The Raven, Ulalume, Annabel Lee di Edgar Allen Poe, nella traduzione di Fernando Pessoa* (Turin: Einaudi, 1955).

11 *Poesie di T.S. Eliot*, trans. Luigi Berti (Parma: Guanda, 1949); T.S. Eliot, *Opere 1904–1939*, ed. R. Sanesi (Milan: Bompiani, 1992).

12 T.S. Eliot, *Poèmes, 1910–1930: Texte anglais présenté et traduit par Pierre Leyris* (Paris: Seuil, 1947).

13 At most it is possible, even over the telephone, given a code that both parties understand, to transmit instructions for the reconstruction of the musical score of the *Fifth*. But this would be a case of mere transcription, as happens with Morse code.

14 Even though in Nordic languages substantives are not as identified with gender as they are in Italian, and, for masculine nouns that do not indicate persons, the personal pronoun for masculine objects or animals, *den*, is used in preference to the masculine personal pronoun, *han*, it nevertheless seems natural that Bergmann tended to 'see' Death as male.

15 For this point, again see Steiner, chapter 6, *passim*.

16 The circumstance acts at most in helping us to consider a succession of dots and dashes as a message in Morse rather than a random arrangement of characters owing to typing errors.

17 After this text of mine was already completed, I saw the proofs of Petrilli 2000. Petrilli mentions the same example and comes to the same conclusions. This strikes me as being in contrast with her tendency to identify 'translation' in its widest sense, à la Jakobson. In fact, Petrilli proposes a classification of the various forms of 'translation' that is more complex than mine (in the sense that it considers subspecies like the passage from oral to written, between various stylistic registers, between standard language and dialect, etc.), but that might be wholly compatible with mine, were it not for the fact that it does not deal with a typology of interpretations but of translations.

18 For my translation, see *Esercizi di stile* (Turin: Einaudi, 1983).

19 The greater redundancy of the target text was part of the challenge: I tended to avoid the *e* in a greater number of words than the original.

20 'Anna Livia Plurabella,' *Prospettive* iv, 2, iv, 11–12, 1940. This version contained interpolations by Ettore Settanni. A first version, which sprang from the collaboration between Joyce and Nino Frank, dated 1938, was edited by Jacqueline Risset in Joyce, *Scritti italiani* (Milano: Mondadori, 1979). The Italian version, the French one, the original text, and other subsequent versions are now in Joyce, *Anna Livia Plurabelle*, ed. Rosa Maria Bollettieri Bosinelli (Turin: Einaudi, 1996), with my introduction.

21 'Anna Livia Plurabelle,' *La Nouvelle Revue Française* xix, 212, 1931. Even though FrJoyce translated from the 1928 version of 'Anna Livia' and ItJoyce

from the definitive 1939 version, there are no important variations regarding the points I intend to mention.

22 For the complete list (perhaps greater than the one imagined by Joyce) and the story of the subsequent growth of the list, from version to version, see Louis O. Mink, *A 'Finnegans Wake' Gazetteer* (Bloomington: Indiana UP, 1968). For the same topic, see also Fred H. Higginson, *Anna Livia Plurabelle: The Making of a Chapter* (Minneapolis: U of Minnesota P, 1960).

23 FrJoyce, for example, gains the Somme, Avon, Niger, Yangtsé, Gironde, Aare, Damève (Danube?), Po, and Saône.

24 No one can maintain that it was not possible to say, for example: 'non sambra che eufrate Dniepro ponesse la rava a sinistra e a destra, con gran senna, nel suo poder ...'

25 'For coxyt sake' also sounds remarkably like 'for coxitis' ache.' Coxitis is a painful inflammation of the hip joint and thus, arguably, a 'pain in the ass.'

26 I would point out that this use of the term 'parasynonymy' is broader than the one put forward by Greimas-Courtès in *Dictionnaire raisonné*.

27 See *The Betrothed*, trans. Bruce Penman (Harmondsworth: Penguin, 1972).

28 *Les fiancés*, trans. Yves Branca (Paris: Gallimard, 1995).

29 See the analysis of the pictorial adaptations of the character of the Nun of Monza in Calabrese 1989. For the visual adaptations of the novel, see also Casetti 1989.

30 Personal communication.

Bibliography

Baker, Mona, ed. 1998. *Routledge Encyclopedia of Translation Studies*. London: Routledge.

Barthes, Roland. 1964. 'Eléments de semiologie.' *Communications* 4. (English trans. *Elements of Semiology*. London: Cape, 1967.)

Basso, Pier Luigi. 1999. 'Fenomenologia della traduzione intersemiotica.' *Versus* 85/86.

Benjamin, Walter. 1923. 'Die Aufgabe des Übersetzers.' Introduction to a translation of Ch. Baudelaire, *Tableaux Parisiens*. Heidelberg. (English trans. in *Delos* 2, 1968.)

Bettetini, G., A. Grasso, and L. Tettamanzi, eds. 1990. *Le mille e una volta dei Promessi Sposi*. Rome: Rai VQPT-Nuova Eri.

Brower, Reuben A., ed. 1959. *On Translation*. Cambridge: Harvard UP.

Calabrese, Omar. 1989. 'L'iconologia della Monaca di Monza.' In *Leggere i 'Promessi Sposi'.* Ed. G. Manetti. Milan: Bompiani.

Cano, Cristina, and Giorgio Cremonini. 1990. *Cinema e musica: Racconto per sovrapposizioni*. Florence: Vallecchi.

Casetti, Francesco. 1989. 'La pagina come schermo: La dimensione visiva nei *Promessi Sposi*.' In *Leggere i 'Promessi Sposi'.* Ed. G. Manetti. Milan: Bompiani.

Derrida, Jacques. 1985. 'Des tours de Babel.' In *Differences in Translation*. Ed. J. Graham. Ithaca: Cornell UP.

Dusi, Nicola. 1998. 'Tra letteratura e cinema: Ritmo e spazialità in "Zazie dans le métro."' *Versus* 80/81.

– 1999. *Da un medium all'altro: La traduzione intersemiotica del senso e degli affetti*. Tesi di Dottorato in Semiotica, A.A. 1999–2000. Università di Bologna.

Eco, Umberto. 1975. *Trattato di semiotica generale*. Milan: Bompiani. (English version. *A Theory of Semiotics*. Bloomington: Indiana UP, 1976.)

– 1977. 'The Influence of Roman Jakobson in the Development of Semiotics.'

In *Roman Jakobson: Echoes of His Scholarship*. Ed. D. Armstrong and C.H. van Schooneveld. Lisse: De Ridder.

‒ 1979. *The Role of the Reader*. Bloomington: Indiana UP. (Also London: Hutchinson, 1981.)

‒ 1980. *Il nome della rosa*. Milan: Bompiani (English trans. *The Name of the Rose*. New York: Harcourt, Brace and Jovanovich, 1983.)

‒ 1985. *Sugli specchi e altri saggi*. Milan: Bompiani.

‒ 1988. *Il pendolo di Foucault*. Milan: Bompiani. (English trans. *Foucault's Pendulum*. New York: Harcourt, Brace and Jovanovich, 1989.)

‒ 1990. *I limiti dell'interpretazione*. Milan: Bompiani. (English trans. *The Limits of Interpretation*. Bloomington: Indiana UP, 1990.)

‒ 1993. *La ricerca della lingua perfetta*. Bari: Laterza. (English trans. *The Quest for a Perfect Language*. Oxford: Blackwell, 1995.)

‒ 1994. *L'isola del giorno prima*. Milan: Bompiani. (English trans. *The Island of the Day Before*. New York: Harcourt Brace 1995.)

‒ 1994. *Six Walks in the Fictional Woods*. Cambridge: Harvard UP.

‒ 1997. *Kant e l'ornitorinco*. Milan: Bompiani. (English trans. *Kant and the Platypus*. New York: Harcourt Brace, 1999.)

Even-Zohar, Itamar, ed. 1990. 'Polysystems Studies.' *Poetics Today* 11, no. 1.

Even-Zohar, I., and G. Tury, eds. 1981. 'Translation Theory and Intercultural Relations.' *Poetics Today* 2, no. 4.

Fabbri, Paolo. 1998. *La svolta semiotica*. Bari: Laterza.

Folena, Gianfranco. 1991. *Volgarizzare e tradurre*. Turin: Einaudi.

Goodman, Nelson. 1968. *Languages of Art*. New York: Bobbs-Merrill.

Gorlée, Dinda. 1994. *Semiotics and the Problem of Translation*. Amsterdam-Atlanta: Rodopi.

Hjelmslev, Louis. 1943. *Prolegomena to a Theory of Language*. Madison: Wisconsin UP.

Jakobson, Roman. 1959. 'On Linguistic Aspects of Translation.' In Brower 1959.

‒ 1960. 'Closing Statements: Linguistics and Poetics.' In *Style in Language*. Ed. T.A. Sebeok. Cambridge: MIT Press.

‒ 1977. 'A Few Remarks on Peirce.' *Modern Language Notes* 93, pp. 1026–36.

Joyce, James. 1996. *Anna Livia Plurabelle*. Ed. Rosa Maria Bosinelli. Turin: Einaudi.

Lepschy, Giulio C. 1981. 'Traduzione'. In *Enciclopedia* 14. Turin: Einaudi.

Mason, Ian. 1998. 'Communicative/Functional Approaches'. In Baker 1998, pp. 29–33.

Nergaard, Siri. 1995. 'Introduzione.' In *Teorie contemporanee della traduzione*. Ed. S. Nergaard. Milan: Bompiani.

Pareyson, Luigi. 1954. *Estetica*. Turin: Edizioni di 'Filosofia' (now Milan: Bompiani 1988).

Peirce, Charles S. 1931–48. *Collected Papers*. Cambridge: Harvard UP.

Petrilli, Susan. 2000. Introduction to *La traduzione*. Special issue of *Athanor* 10, no. 2 (1999–2000).

Quine, Willard Van Orman. 1960. *Word and Object*. Cambridge: MIT Press.

Rustico, Carmelo. 1999. *Il tema dell'estetica in Peirce*. Tesi di Laurea, AA 1998–9, Università di Bologna.

Savan, David. 1988. *An Introduction to C.S. Peirce's Full System of Semeiotic*. Monograph Series of the Toronto Semiotic Circle, No. 1.

Schäffner, Christina. 1998. 'Skopos Theory.' In Baker 1998, pp. 235–8.

Steiner, George. 1975. *After Babel*. London: Oxford UP.

Venuti, Lawrence. 1998. 'Strategies of Translation.' In Baker 1998, pp. 240–4.

Wittgenstein, Ludwig. 1966. *Lectures and Conversations on Aesthetics, Psychology and Religious Belief*. Oxford: Blackwell.